10-Minute

Kid Clutter
Control

10-Minute
Kid Clutter Control

Hundreds of Proven Tips Even Kids Can Do!

ROSE R. KENNEDY

FAIR WINDS
PRESS
GLOUCESTER, MASSACHUSETTS

Text ©2006 by Fair Winds Press

First published in the USA in 2006 by
Fair Winds Press, a member of
Quayside Publishing Group
33 Commercial Street
Gloucester, MA 01930

10 09 08 07 06   1 2 3 4 5

ISBN 1-59233-224-2

Library of Congress Cataloging-in-Publication Data available

Original cover design by Laura Shaw
Book design by *tabula rasa* graphic design
Cover Illustration by Elizabeth Cornaro

Printed and bound in USA

To Wade, my partner in the clutter-cutting battle,

in the hope that love conquers all.

CONTENTS

How to Use This Book

THIS BOOK IS DIVIDED INTO THREE PARTS. PART ONE, "Getting Started", tells you how to manage household clutter at all different stages of your child's life. Part Two, "One Area at a Time," provides quick and easy clutter-clearing projects and ideas for each room of the home. For those families whose various hobbies threaten to overtake the entire house, Part Three, "Outside Interests (and the Stuff They Spawn)," will help you manage the mess in a way you never thought possible.

To give this book a broader range of expertise, many of the ideas inside were taken from "everyday experts," people who have used them successfully in their own businesses and homes, from troop leaders to professional organizers to family counselors. Some of the tactics are ones I've had personal success with helping my kids grow up into the reasonably organized teenagers they are today. Others I only wish I'd had at my disposal when my kids were younger.

Be on the lookout for these specialized tips appearing throughout the book!

 ## Clutter Busting Basics

Fundamental, everyday principles for maintaining a clutter-free home.

10 Minutes of Prevention

Quick and easy ways to stop clutter before it starts.

 When Clutter Enablers Strike

Polite and effective ways to handle kids, relatives, and others who (usually unknowingly) aid and abet kid clutter.

 Clear Thinking

These tips will help keep you in a clutter control mindset, despite popular myths and prevailing pack-rat philosophies.

 "I Can Do It Myself"

Products and equipment that help kids do their own clutter-busting.

Introduction

UNTIL MY TWO DAUGHTERS WERE TODDLERS, I LIVED WITH my husband in the same house he grew up in. I vividly remember my newlywed horror when I rifled through a kitchen drawer for a can opener and came up with five assorted shoe polishes, three polishing cloths—one of them used—and a container of mink oil. John was genuinely perplexed at my reaction. "That's where my family has always kept the shoe polish so we can polish our shoes on the kitchen table!" he remarked good-naturedly. "It's going to be hard to do it differently thirty years later!"

Changing the way you organize and move about your household is a challenge no matter how long you've been doing things the same way. But the payoffs are innumerable, for every member of the family. Some are obvious—your house looks cleaner, Susie can find her homework in the morning, and you're not paying for duplicate can openers, Scotch tape, and jars of mustard all the time. Mom and Dad can also decompress more quickly after a hard day of work in a home with less "visual stress."

But there's something bigger that's bound to happen once you begin to clear the clutter. A gradual shift in attitude accompanies diminishing piles of stuff: Pleasant space becomes more important than having the latest gadget or a closet floor full of fashionable clothes. As a family, you'll begin to contemplate what you have, what you need, and how you can help others by sharing the things that you don't need. And you as a parent start to sharpen a skill you'll need often in the years ahead: knowing when to hold on tight, and when to let go.

This book will show you how to make your home more pleasant while instilling clutter-clearing habits in your children, from as early an age as you can catch them. You'll be amazed at how much your kids will benefit from being involved.

In the course of researching this book, I was struck by the way organization expert Monica Ricci, of Atlanta, summed up the process: "When kids take charge of their spaces and possessions, it teaches them pride of ownership and gives them an investment in the care and maintenance of their home. They have a sense of responsibility and accomplishment that will stay with them the rest of their lives." A decluttered household, like a love of reading or good manners, is in reach for your child as long as you're interested in promoting it—a fine luxury you can provide regardless of your income, family situation, or which area of the world you live in.

Not all of the expert tips that follow will work with your specific organizing style or household, so feel free to pick and choose among the most useful. At this house, for example, we no longer keep shoe polish in the kitchen, but we do have plastic army men on the hall bookshelf and the heirloom quilts stored in the same armoire as the stereo.

The one idea which I hope you'll take to heart, whatever

your circumstances, is that you can do this soul-satisfying clearing ten minutes at a time. No matter how busy you are or how hopeless all those piles of stuff make you feel, you can make a significant dent in the clutter by focusing a small chunk of your time on the problem at hand. So let's get started . . . there's nothing to lose but the clutter!

Rose R. Kennedy

Rose R. Kennedy

PART ONE

Getting Started

Chapter One

MAKE UP YOUR MINDSET

EVER SEE THIS SIGN IN SOMEONE'S OFFICE? "IF A CLUTTERED DESK IS THE sign of a cluttered mind, what does an empty desk mean?"

Jokes aside, clutter, particularly kid's clutter, has everything to do with the way you think. Some long-held beliefs and ingrained habits may open the door to more clutter or make it tougher to clear what's already gotten a foothold in the household. Ten minutes spent squaring away outdated ideas that contribute to clutter could be just as beneficial as the same time spent clearing a cabinet.

Here are some mindsets that encourage clutter, along with more encouraging ways to think about things:

CLUTTER BUG MINDSET #1

"I'm saving it for a rainy day."

So many of us have parents or grandparents who grew up in the Depression, and that "save everything" feeling has persevered long after it's no longer necessary. It's a great temptation to hold onto everything from sleeping bags (when we don't camp) to second refrigerators to extra copies of Scrabble "just in case" it comes in handy down the road.

This mindset also leads people to stock up on things that they don't really need. My brother-in-law, Rob Stanford, who is a chef in Tampa, points out that people still shop for food to keep on hand "if there's a natural disaster or unexpected guests," as if there's not a grocery store less than a mile away that's open late.

Reality is, none but the most isolated rural folks need to buy more food than they can eat in a week, and absolutely no one needs anything they haven't used in a year, unless it's an heirloom. Whether it's big, like the crib you keep in the attic in case someone in the extended family needs it later, or small, like the extra packet of bacon bits you bought because they were two for one, stuff you're not using now is a major clutter culprit.

So how do you shuck off this "saver" mentality? Constantly remind yourself, and your kids, **"someone else could be making better use of this right now and who knows if we'll ever use it?"** and **"We might need this later, but we need space right now!"**

CLUTTER BUG MINDSET #2

"We can't afford to get organized."

Oh, the lure of all those nifty interlocking plastic tubs and custom-designed revolving shelves! They cost hundreds, maybe thousands, of dollars, but the truth is: They are a fun extra, not a fundamental decluttering tool.

If you'll take the time, ten minutes at a time, to sort and throw out, you will accomplish loads without spending anything more than the cost of retrieving some empty cardboard boxes and the gas expended driving discards to Goodwill. Later, if you want to, invest in some nice stuff or those built-in cabinets. But make sure you make the "for free" efforts first—and never let the prospect of paying out down the road keep you from starting now. That would be like worrying how you'd ever pay the income tax if you won $10 million in the lottery! Figure that out when it becomes an issue!

CLUTTER BUG MINDSET #3

"If I can't control my own clutter, how can I expect it from the kids!"

I won't let my children say that they're "stupid," or drink more caffeine than is contained in a half can of soda. But for myself . . . let's just say I've already got a few bad habits.

It's the same way with your kid's clutter. Don't feel like a hypocrite if they've got drawers full of clean and coordinated clothes that fit—and only the clothes that fit—and you can't even find a pair of pantyhose without a run before you leave for work. Instead, remind yourself that **you want your kids to have the best home environment you can offer them,** which is why you're tackling their clutter before you've mastered your own.

Don't let your own clutter failures stop you from trying anew with for your kids. Think of putting up with your mother-in-law, going to Chuck E. Cheese, quitting smoking—how many things will you do for your kids' benefit that you won't do just to benefit yourself? If you need to, make decluttering one of them.

In areas where your clutter intersects, like the family room or bathroom, you'll all benefit from the kid-oriented efforts. **Once you realize you can declutter the kid areas, you may gain enough confidence to tackle your own things,** and a lot of the same methods will apply.

CLUTTER BUG MINDSET #4

"I want my kids to have the best of everything."

All the pediatric books I read when my oldest daughter was two said not to overwhelm a child with too-large food portions, but I would constantly come home to my husband serving up a two-cup serving of macaroni and cheese, or, more than once, an entire bunch of steamed broccoli that looked like a shrub clutched in her small hand. He wasn't defying the doctor, he just wanted to make sure his child knew she had plenty of everything—and all he had to offer.

This is an endearing attitude from either parent, at any income level, but it can really get you into trouble clutter-wise. It's too easy, especially if you feel like you were deprived in your own childhood, or maybe can't spend as much time with your kids as you would like, to buy everything in multiples—from skirts to CDs to breakfast cereals.

And it's a difficult mindset to shift, but keep reminding yourself, **"this isn't about saving money, or how much I love my child, it's about space."** By keeping purchases to a chosen few and constantly culling the excess, you and your child will get more enjoyment from the things you have—and from your time together.

If you're one of those parents who's kind of competitive about your child having the latest thing, remind yourself that tranquil spaces and a well-organized home are luxuries much more difficult to procure than the latest video games, and much more beneficial to your child. And if in the final analysis you just can't help feeling like a cheapskate if you don't indulge your child, try buying better quality over quantity, or emphasizing events—like concerts or a cooking class taken together—over purchases.

CLUTTER BUG MINDSET #5

"My kids are too young to worry about clutter."

I think clutter-cutting is like a foreign language—much easier to pick up in your formative years. Like everything we do as parents, the idea is to do for the kids until they can do for themselves, whether it's presenting healthy food choices or enforcing a time out when they throw a tantrum.

In clutter terms, that means before children can walk and talk, simplifying possessions is the parents' responsibility. But once kids are about two years old, they can sort socks like a pro, and at any age after they can become a part of keeping clutter out of the house.

Keep in mind, too, that the possessions you amass in your child's preschool and elementary years can easily snowball. If you don't curb clutter from the start, you'll have a harder time reclaiming some pleasant living areas when your kid's a pre-teen. So try to establish good clutter habits early——for your child's development and to make future decluttering easier.

CLUTTER BUG MINDSET #6

"My kids are too old—I've missed my chance to help them with clutter."

It's never too late. If your kid didn't pick up the knack as a youngster, all it takes is some extra effort on your part to get them up to speed. Like balancing a checkbook or driving defensively, **the ability to organize living spaces and simplify possessions is something you don't want to send your child into the world without.**

CLUTTER BUG MINDSET #7

"I hate to ruin our time together as a family."

If they've never helped out much around the house, you probably will meet some resistance from your kids when you decide you're going to do some decluttering. Your spouse may also resist clean-up time after a long, hard day, and of course it's hard to work up your own motivation, too.

But don't let that hold you back! There are plenty of ideas in this book for getting you and your family motivated, especially when you're only asking for ten minutes at a time. And here's the interesting part: While you're fretting that the kids will hate going through boxes instead of going to a movie, you might overlook that sometimes it's fun to check out your old stuff together. You might share a memory, have an impromptu dress-up session or share a laugh over the things you've held on to. "What is this salad spinner thingie?" or "Did you honestly think I might wear this to a prom some day?" You may discover that working together as a family somehow becomes good, old-fashioned quality time.

But **the greatest benefit is having clear spaces for play, thought and time together . . .** which makes all your family's time spent decluttering time well spent.

Chapter Two

BABY STEPS

BEFORE BABY ARRIVES, IT'S UP TO YOU TO SET THE STAGE FOR A TRANQUIL, streamlined home. And once they're walking and talking? Hoo boy. A few simple strategies during the infant to pre-Kindergarten years will stem the tide of excess stuff, and prevent lots of clutter later.

Before baby, set the simplified standard.

You're expecting and everybody's thrilled, whether it's your first little darling or the finale for a blended family with six kids already.

In the beginning, despite all those overwhelming nursery lists they give you at the baby super store, your baby needs very little: clothes, food, diapers, a place to sleep, a place to rock, and some bedding. Anything beyond that and you're inviting clutter and creating visual stress for the tired people who will be tending the newborn. "For the first few months, the baby herself won't be real aware of her surroundings," says Steve Brown, a licensed clinical social worker based in Knoxville, Tennessee. "But the new parents need a soothing environment for nursing, putting the child to sleep, and bonding. Too much junk in the nursery has a negative effect on the family's environment."

While some people don't believe in the benefits of playing classical music to the unborn baby, there is a clear advantage to establishing good clutter habits in the womb. It's one of the few times you'll be in complete charge of your child's possessions, and if you start her life with little clutter, you'll have less cumulative clutter and also a simplified standard from the start.

When Clutter Enablers Strike

Handle baby gift givers with kid gloves.

It is usually a good idea to stem the tide of unnecessary baby products before it's too late. Besides, handling folks bearing baby gifts is good training for handling future meddling in your child's discipline and eating habits. You must be diplomatic but still get the message across, "We prefer just to have a few things for the baby." Explain to people who ask what you want for the baby either that, "We're overwhelmed by all this stuff and would just like to request your well wishes for now," or "We already have all the items our doctor recommended, so now we're just saving for the crib (high chair, car seat) that we want." The most well-meaning people might take your hint and offer to chip in.

When Clutter Enablers Strike

Get the grandparents on your side.

If one of the sets of grandparents is feeling like the best way to stay involved is with big gifts of nonessentials, remember to remind them that what you want most is for them to really get to know the baby and spend some time with her. If they still want to throw some money around and you're close enough to have such a conversation, ask for contributions to the baby's college fund.

Ask for disposable diapers.

It's a blast to shop for an infant, even when he hasn't been born yet. Don't rob family members and friends of all their pleasure, but if you know a whole lot of people are going to be buying presents for the babe, gently suggest a disposable diaper shower if you want to avoid misguided gifts that could hang around the house forever. Babies go through astonishing numbers of diapers, so there's no danger that big boxes full will be lurking when your child's ready to start kindergarten. But don't be tacky about the whole thing: remember, you just let really close friends or the person throwing the shower know your wishes, and grin and bear it when everyone gets you silver brushes and weird wall art instead.

Clear Thinking

Buy duplicates of baby clothes you like.

The accounting department at my husband's office threw us a shower when I was expecting my first child. Boy was I surprised to open a package with four identical dark blue "onesies" inside. "They're all the same!" I exclaimed. "That's so you'll actually get a chance to see the baby in the outfit!" said the gift giver, a new mom herself. She was right, too—any of my favorite outfits on the baby were always changed to something else within a half-hour of dolling her up (they tend to spit up on the ones you like most). Buying multiples of the clothes you really like has two clutter benefits: they're easier to sort, you won't need as many clothes to keep the baby in an outfit that matches, and, most importantly, when you're deciding which outfits to hang onto for sentimental reasons, you can get rid of one (or two, or three) and hold on to the other.

Resist buying infant care sets.

I was so tickled with the comb that came in a "grooming" set someone had purchased for my oldest daughter before she was born . . . because for the first six months of her life, she had absolutely no hair! That's the trouble with the "gift sets" amassed by clever retailers—you never really know what parts of it you'll want or need. Not everyone uses baby powder or baby wash, for example, but they're standard equipment in a baby bathing set. For clutter's sake, buy all bathing and grooming items separately, and in small quantities, until you're sure what brand and what products you'll really use.

Borrow the basics or shop at thrift stores.

Not only will you save money when you buy used changing tables
or high chairs, but you'll feel less compelled to hang onto them for
years afterward. After all, that changing table from Goodwill is no one's
idea of a family heirloom. It's also easier to think of putting the items
back into the giveaway arena when that's where they came from in the
first place.

Keep prelabeled boxes and packing tape on hand.

Infants and toddlers grow so fast and can change so much in the space of a few months. That means you'll have a constant stream of toys, clothes, and such to send to a younger child. If you put it off for too long, that younger child might outgrow the stuff before it arrives! To increase your chances of staying on top of the giveaways, keep a sturdy box on hand and label it ahead of time with the name and address of the people you usually swap stuff with. Set a roll of packing tape inside and keep it in the nursery, so you can place giveaways directly in the box. Once it's full, seal it up and mail it off. Start a new box that very same day!

Clear Thinking

Toddlers shouldn't be collectors.

Now that the baby's old enough to have preferences, it's really tempting to run out and buy her the whole set of Pretty Ponies, or seven shapes of macaroni. But the fact is, a small child can only play with one toy at once, and doesn't need to be overwhelmed with more. If you turn them into collectors at this early stage, just imagine how overcrowded your house will become!

Rotate your toddler's toys.

Once your baby can walk and talk, he's going to be ready for more "stuff," from toys and games to movies, clothes, shoes, and so on. The best trick for keeping toddler clutter under control is to rotate the stock. Put out just a few toys at a time, or keep a few DVDs at the ready and store the rest out of sight. For a developing toddler, something he hasn't seen in a few weeks is "new," and for his tired parents, just a few toys out at a time makes it easier to clean, organize, and put everything away at the end of the day. And if you make sure things in the "out of sight" box are in good shape, they'll be ready for giveaway if your child outgrows them before the next rotation.

Don't do duplicates.

If there's a toy or video your tot loves at Grandma's or preschool, let
them enjoy it there! Resist the temptation to buy a duplicate for the
house—that's one too many of even the most popular toy. And you
may find that part of the reason the child likes the toy so much is she
only gets to have it at Grandma's. The same applies if your children
have divorced parents: Although you want them to have around the
same amount of fun stuff at both places, there's no point in buying a
game they already use at the other parent's home. The exception to this
duplication rule is when two children in the same family are deeply
attached to a toy or book. Then it makes sense to provide each with her
own copy of *Runaway Bunny* or Polly Pocket's townhouse. There will
always be exceptions, but in general try to stick to one of a toy or one
set of stuff, like Tinkertoys or Legos.

Teach little ones to sort.

Part of a preschooler's "work" is learning to identify shapes and similarities through play. To give them the expectation that life implicitly involves organizing and sorting from an early age, let them try some simple organizing tasks—preferably ones you really need done, not "made up" jobs. Pairing colored socks is one idea, and sorting cans from the pictures on the labels is another.

Choose for your child.

Before a child is four or so, it's a futile exercise to ask him which toys and books he's ready to give away. Just as you've probably noticed the idea of sharing doesn't come naturally to toddlers, they won't really understand that you're asking them to choose one game over another and that the other one will be "gone." Instead, use your own observations about which toys your child is playing with a lot, and enlist the opinions of other caregivers and even older children before deciding which kid stuff to part with.

Give a toddler time to change your mind.

Create an out of sight "holding area" for toddler items you're getting ready to give away and see if your child asks for the toy in the next week or so. The busy mind of a two-year-old means they sometimes recall something they want quite badly, even when it's been out of sight for a while, but after a week, you're usually safe.

Chapter Three

SCHOOL DAYS

O NCE YOUR CHILD'S NO LONGER IN YOUR EXCLUSIVE CARE, HE'LL BE A
conduit for clutter from the outside world, from school to activities and well-meaning friends. But you can still arm your child with
good habits and kindly phrases to keep "stuff" from pouring into the
house or gaining a stronghold once it's indoors.

Create a Big Gift Rule.

Make it a family rule that a child has to check first before accepting anything bigger than a deck of cards. Sure, this might occasionally make you the bad guy, but it's a graceful way to turn down castoffs, while you still leave the door open on things you really need or your child really covets. It's also easy to use because it doesn't take a lot of judgment on your child's part: "Is this bigger than a deck of cards? Yes." Once you've tried it a few times, the habit may still seem a little odd to friends and relatives, but it will become automatic and takes care of unwanted objects from the plastic sword your six-year-old's new school friend "gave" him to the big box of castoff clothes your daughter would otherwise lug home from after-school care. Have your child practice with you at home first, saying, "That's a nice offer, but I always have to check with my mom first because it's bigger than a deck of cards. No, that's just our rule. It looks great to me, but we may not be able to keep it." Another benefit of this strategy is that in the time it takes to double check with a parent, the offer may expire or the child may forget all about, say, that giant stuffed animal the neighbor had for free at her yard sale.

I Can Do It Myself

Provide your kids with step stools.

That upper shelf is the best place for items your child doesn't use every day, from swimsuits to dress-up clothes. But it's not a good way to encourage organization and responsibility if only Mom or Dad can reach what's up there. By giving your child a step stool, you'll enable them to get things and put things away on their own and you'll get more use out of higher shelves and closet rods.

Clutter-Cutting Basics

Try to keep up with your child's changing needs and tastes.

Here's another example of how the clutter-cutting process can make you a better parent—and how it utilizes skills you've picked up along with your parenting responsibilities. To keep from pumping unwanted or unusable objects into the household, make every attempt to keep up with your child's changing likes and dislikes, from clothes and food to hobbies and entertainment. I know I was buying a certain brand of spinach noodles for my daughter years after she's stopped liking them, and Wade lovingly decorated his 8th grade daughter's room when she was gone for spring break in Sponge Bob posters, at least a few months after she'd started burying her Sponge Bob comforter beneath the other blankets to hide it from public view. Considering things in clutter terms—"Does Sue still need a hundred different Beanie Babies in this tiny bedroom?"—may help you adjust to the fact that your baby is forever changing and growing up.

Sort at the door.

Now that you have so many agents bringing paperwork and other stuff in the house, make sure any that's unneeded stops at the door——literally. Set a trash can and a mixed paper recycle box near whichever entrance the kids come through at the end of the day, and have them pause to toss and sort for a minute or two before proceeding into the house. Just as important, take those trash bags with you regularly as you leave the house, or make it someone's job to empty them when they reach a certain mark.

Create money packets for school expenses.

A parent's busy morning usually includes gathering money for their child's lunch or bus fare. Don't waste time and create clutter with lots of little piles of ones and change throughout the house, none of which seems to contain the amount you need in the morning. Here's a great job for kids just learning to count change or older kids learning the value of saving: At the beginning of the week, help them make portions of the required fees and wrap them (bills and change together) in small foil packets. Use a market to label them. My favorite has always been to use the inner foil liners from sugarless peppermint gum, but my kids tell me I'm a little weird and ordinary bits of aluminum foil will work just as well. Put the packets in an easy-to-reach flat bowl or small basket and you're all set. This will also save you a bit of money if you keep up with the habit, because it's a lot harder to unwrap several packets of bus fare than it is to scoop up a handful of quarters when you hear the ice cream man. Just make sure someone checks the supply midway through the week to make sure you're not caught short later.

Clear Thinking

You don't have to be a well organized adult to encourage good school paper habits.

No matter that you've got cascades of mail order catalogs under your bed or have not returned a music club "Pick of the Month" on time since the '90s—you can still keep your child's school stuff organized, whether she's starting this year or has been at it a while. No one has to know about your secret clutter life, all they'll see is your streamlined approach to your kid's paperwork. And your child won't pick up on the discrepancy either, because he'll consider school papers a natural extension of that very organized place known as his classroom.

Clutter-Cutting Basics

Set an expiration date for school paperwork and stick to it.

Keep homework, report cards and other paper-related school items in a crate, box, or upright file for each child so it will all be handy in one place. But here's the trick: Instead of duplicating efforts by going back through these papers every so often, establish a system where you plan each paper's fate the first time you file it. That means different files labeled "Child A, First Grade, Keep," "Child A, First Grade, Toss After January 2008" and so forth. Then, the very first time a report card goes into the file, it's already in the "Keep" folder. Your copy of that permission slip for the April field trip? It stays for now, but only in a file with a planned "toss" date. To really make this approach work, though, stick to the file names—don't sort back through the files that say "toss" to reconsider.

Install in/out boxes for school paperwork.

If you can lick the barrage of permission slips, report cards, and gift wrap sales literature that follows your child home from school every day, you'll have conquered around half the kid clutter generated in these years—and helped your child's school performance at the same time. One sensible option is an "in/out" box attached to a wall within easy reach of both parents and children, placed strategically above the cubbies or hooks where you park backpacks. A transparent office-paper sorter is about ten bucks at an office supply store, and you should mount it at eye level for the child. Label one slot for parents to look at and one slot for things kids need to turn back in. Make sure you use sheetrock screws, because it entirely defeats the purpose if the sorter won't stay on the wall.

Reward them for a job well done.

This is easier if you're starting with a kindergartener, but you can also get an older kid in the habit of sorting and delivering school forms and homework. Just make sure to let the teacher know you're trying hard to work with this method, and then reinforce by occasionally leaving treats for your child in the folder, either at home or at school. One other tactic: Run spot checks on your child's back pack to make sure the right papers are in the take home folder, and give him a small reward if everything's where it should be.

I Can Do It Myself

Try a see-through file for take home papers.
A lot of teachers designate one folder for "take home" stuff,
whether that means approval forms or the night's science
homework. If they don't, you can, but try to make it a see-
through folder that's sturdy and can be wiped off. That way
you can easily see if your kid brought home something you
need to see, and your child—and her teacher—can easily see
if you sent back what you needed to. More important than
the see-through factor, though, is constantly using the folder—
both you and the child.

Four Ways to Keep Computer Files Organized.

Although they're actually inside the computer, files for homework and fun can be a sort of "virtual" clutter if they're not organized. Here are four ways to keep it under control from computer experts, including Carl Slate from Willliamsburg, Virginia, father of three young adults and grandfather to four young children.

1. Make separate spaces on the disk drive for each member of the family who uses the computer. "For Windows XP operating systems, each person has their own account and their own root My Document folder," says Carl. "But when your operating system only can handle one user account, create a user folder for each family member within the My Documents folder. This makes all user documents easier to find because they are all in one place. It also keeps the clutter down on the rest of your computer." If you don't know how, consult the manual, the 800- help number for your computer or word processing program, or attend computer classes often offered through the library or local night school.

2. Organize within user folders. "An adult may want to start by creating three folders in their root user directory such as 'Personal,' 'Business' and 'Other' while a student might need 'Friends,' 'School,' and 'Other,'" says Carl. "I like to keep an 'Other' folder for the stuff that you are not sure where to put. All other folders should be based on the major interests of the individual user or the way an individual user views the world."

3. If they're old enough to save files, they're old enough to type a name and date. Have everyone put a sensible two word description of the document in its title, followed by the month and year it was created. This makes it easier to figure out if you can trash it, and also to run a search with keywords to find it if gets misplaced.

4. Create perishable folders. Start folders, for, say "5th grade math" and then label them with the date they'll be obsolete, "delete 01 08." Just as you would with paper folders, don't go back and see what needs saving after the "delete by" date—just do it.

Send an e-mail.

Once your child's old enough to use e-mail to keep in touch with friends and relatives, consider it for internal communications, too. A quick "remember I need to bring $18 for photos tomorrow" doesn't take any paper or pen at all. Plus, if you both know that important communications are coming over the e-mail, you'll be more likely to check it often. If you can't check e-mail frequently, though, the extra clutter from the paper trail is still your best option.

Don't save big graphics or music files.

Instead, once that picture of Thomas Jefferson has been printed out for the 3rd grade report, delete it, and ditto for any music you or the kids have already downloaded to the MP3 player. You don't need two copies, and weeding through all those files every time you want a current document is exhausting.

When Clutter Enablers Strike

Give kids a choice of clutter-clearing activities.

To increase their confidence and hone their decision-making skills, young kids do need to have some age-appropriate decisions regarding their clutter-cutting activities, and you can provide them—just make sure they're real choices. A few examples: "Would you rather sort the socks or the T-shirts?" or "Do you think you can handle the ten thing rule today, or are you feeling good enough to try twenty?" Don't disguise consequences or your hard-felt opinions with options like, "You can get some clutter out of this room or spend the next two days with no phone privileges, it's up to you," or, for younger kids, "Should we sort through this great batch of toys or those icky, greasy tools over there?" You just set yourself up for confrontation if the kid chooses what is clearly—to you the parent at least—the undesirable option. And don't worry, there's so much clutter you'll never be at a loss to give plenty of options for organizing jobs.

Create separate compartments for kids' computer accessories.

Computers attract clutter just as readily as they draw dust, particularly if your kids spend a lot of time typing papers or online. Maryellen Duckett, a full-time freelance writer in Powell, Tennessee, uses a few simple plastic Rubbermaid tubs to corral her three girls' computer accessories. "The computer's in the kitchen and there's not much room. It used to be a problem when one girl would leave a bunch of stuff on the computer and the next would come by and move it and then leave her stuff. Now we use these Rubbermaid plastic tubs that just slide right under the computer desk. When you leave, you put your stuff in your tub and slide it out of sight. If you don't put your history in the tub and now it's gone, that's not anyone else's problem!"

Reinforce school lessons when you cut clutter.

Lots of the lessons learned in school are just begging for reinforcement at home, and clutter cutting provides numerous opportunities. Ask a new reader, for example, to sort the cans in the pantry by the words on the labels, or teach a fourth grader a math application by letting him compute the expiration dates on the dairy products in the fridge. And no one has to tell you how compelling the science lessons are in the areas of the environment and recycling. Reinforce papers your kids bring home or lessons in their text books by cutting some clutter and recycling at the same time. A few good areas for starters include purging magazines, catalogs, and books, taking old newspapers to the dog pound to be reused, and vetting the garage to dispose of some out-of-date products there.

Initiate youngsters to the world of store returns and Ebay.
Once a kid can read and operate the computer for personal gain, it's
time to show him how to make calls when you need to return a product
or grocery that isn't working out. How much clutter in your house con-
sists of items no one took the time to take back to the store? Arm your
child with a different attitude early on, even offering her a 10 percent
cut of the money from the return if it's something like a can of beets or
defective snow boots. Also collaborate with your school-age child when
you sell discards on Ebay. She can probably follow the action online for
you if you show her how, but in any case, the exercise reinforces the
idea that, "We try hard to get the things we can't use to people who
can."

Chapter Four

TEEN CLUTTER

AS YOUR RELATIONSHIP WITH YOUR TEEN GROWS, SO MUST YOUR repertoire of kid clutter-cutting strategies. A teen needs different tools and motivators than her younger siblings—and you'll need to learn when to push and when to let go. But persevere, because learning to deal with clutter is a life skill that will help your teen exert her independence.

Keep your expectations reasonable.

If you and your teen are already sparring over issues of independence and behavior, clutter-cutting is unlikely to be the activity that brings you back to the genial days of Good Ol' Mom and a cooperative nine year old. So anticipate the same sort of results you've been getting on other joint projects, from learning to kayak together to going back-to-school shopping. With some preplanning, you'll improve your odds of success, but it's unlikely to go exactly as you planned. If it's any consolation, it's unlikely to go precisely the way your teen would like, either.

If it's in your teen's room, it's not your clutter.

It took some trial and error, but Shawn Simpson, a former office manager for a group of psychotherapists, finally figured out that she couldn't expect her teen son and daughter to be as organized as she was, but she could require them to keep their stuff where it wouldn't bother her. "For my kids, the key was finding a home for all their stuff in their rooms instead of all over the rest of house," says Shawn, who now lives in Belfair, Washington. "So, baskets, crates, open shelves, and closets with the doors closed worked best. I controlled the rest of the house and they had their space in their rooms. Yes, their rooms looked messy, but I could always close the bedroom doors!"

Encourage them to develop their own system.

"Once children are teenagers, they need to come up with their own system of organization that they're comfortable with, their own methodology," says Molly Kale, center director for a Sylvan Learning Center in Maryville, Tennessee. The teen then informs you of the plan, and the two of you should agree on a specific, measurable indicator that the system is working, whether it's that she's not late for the bus more than one morning every two weeks or that you can't smell his bedroom if you stand in the hall with the door closed. "But you can't be afraid to change it, either," says Molly, who holds a bachelor's degree in education. "Two weeks in, if it's not working, your teen will need to come up with another solution."

Let them pick their own storage containers.

You may salivate at the thought of dozens of interlocking plastic boxes with matching red plastic lids, but that might not suit your teen's style. To help make clutter clearing a bit more creative and fun, give her a budget and let her take the lead in finding storage receptacles that suit her, from floral hat boxes from an estate sale to apple crates, clean or new aluminum pails and trash cans, army/navy surplus backpacks and footlockers, vintage canisters, breadboxes, cookie jars, or lunch boxes. One warning though—just as you would need to sort your stuff before indulging in some new containers for the things you choose to keep, your teen should make some headway with the hard work before making any purchases.

Take away a chore and replace it with an organizing duty.
If your teen already has duties around the house, don't add sorting and organizing (for herself or the household) to the mix without increasing rewards or eliminating other jobs. Why not take away their least favorite chore, like taking out the garbage, and have them help organize the garage for ten minutes every Saturday?

Give lots of choices.

Two of the core strategies outlined by Adele Faber and Elaine Mazlish's in their book *How to Talk So Teens Will Listen and Listen So Teens Will Talk* are to "give choices" and "write it down." Whether you're trying to budge that pile of teen clothing or need help sorting the family's plastic storage containers, combine the two strategies with a written list of ten-minute clutter-cutting jobs. Then ask your teen to choose a fair number and a "due by" date. You may be surprised to find that your child's more interested in, say, sorting through the decade-old baby clothes than doing a self-serving job like discarding old school papers, but you'll never learn your child's preferences if you don't put lots of options out there. Another Faber and Mazlish strategy that's fun: Have your teen jot down ten, ten-minute jobs for you to choose from—reminding him that if it concerns his stuff, he'll have to let you in his room to get the work done!

Appeal to their new sense of self.

The benefits of clutter cutting are the same for you no matter how old your child is—a nicer place to live and relax, less visual stress, cleaner air, less time spent cleaning . . . A teenager, however, sees the benefits of a clean house differently than he did when he was 4 or 8. If you're smart, you can turn his changing attitude to your advantage. For example, your teen might think the following: "A neater house won't embarrass me when I have new friends over, especially that guy (girl) I like" or "Mom's more likely to let me have more friends over if the house isn't as cluttered." Shawn Simpson of Belfair, Washington, also found that her teens became more cooperative in keeping their clothes organized when they started to care about their appearance. "We used lots of large baskets at my house and the kids could toss their clean clothes in them instead of on the floor," she remembers. "If they didn't get their dirty clothes in the only dirty clothes basket in the house, then their clothes didn't get washed. Now, this wouldn't work for some teens, but it worked with mine 'cause they both became very picky about their appearance when they reached high school."

Show them how to make a buck.

If your teen is resistant to learning basic clutter-cutting skills, remind him that people pay good money to have others come sort their junk for them. A teen is every bit as capable of reading the "Basic Skills" chapters of this book as you are—and probably far more motivated to turn any lessons learned into a little cottage industry, sorting and organizing for older neighbors or busy two-earner couples, offering to hold yard sales or sell stuff on Ebay for a percentage of the profits, or to transport items to donation centers for an hourly fee.

Put them in the driver's seat! If your teen's really excited about a new driver's license, that's the person you should designate to take donations and discards to their new homes on a regular basis.

Make magazine recycling fun. Teens are dreamers by definition and get lots of their ideas from magazines and catalogs. Most teens have a stack of old magazines clogging up valuable closet space. Encourage them to relax, put on some good music and spend some 10 minute sessions clipping and filing just the articles and photos they want from old magazines, then recycling the rest right away.

Ten gifts that will slow the tide of teen clutter.

You and your relatives may unwittingly be adding to a teen's clutter by giving them gifts they don't need or that they've outgrown. Instead, consider the following gifts for teens:

1. Money towards sports or dance lessons
2. Concert tickets
3. Sporting event tickets
4. Auto store or gas certificates
5. A stock or bond for a favorite company
6. Pet treats and a pet grooming certificate
7. Membership in AAA or a similar roadside assistance plan
8. A gift certificate for manicure, pedicure, or haircut
9. Prepaid admission for the bowling alley, climbing center, skating rink, or any other active places that can be expensive
10. A personal batch of their favorite cookies.

Give the gift of a good friend.

When your family already pays for most of your teen's discretionary and entertainment expenses, it won't work to start giving gift certificates for the same things in lieu of presents. To keep gifts clutter free, just offer to pay for a friend or date to accompany your child to the same activities you already sponsor. By doing this, you acknowledge that your child is interested in "outside the family" companionship now that he's older, and it also allows him the pleasure of providing for someone else, maybe even an underprivileged buddy.

Make a clutter-free gift jar.

It's sort of like a reverse "job jar." Have your teen write out ten or twelve reasonable substitutes for gifts of "stuff" on slips of paper and put them in a jar. Then, next time there's an occasion or you just want to surprise your high-schooler, dip into the jar and indulge one of the requests. Best of all, you won't be at a loss when puzzled grandparents, aunts, and uncles want to know what the kid wants—and you don't want any more clutter!

Make your own gift certificates.

The formal cards and certificates you purchase from a retailer can become a sort of clutter themselves if your teen amasses enough of them, forgets to use them, or loses them. And if they go out of date before they're redeemed, there goes your investment! Instead, make your own gift certificate for anything but gas or fast food and then take your teen to "redeem" it, paying right there with cash or a credit card. That way, the whole gift-giving experience doesn't deteriorate to the equivalent of your child getting cash and then going out to buy his own gifts.

Chapter Five

TIPS FOR ALL AGES

THERE ARE A FEW TECHNIQUES THAT ARE USEFUL IN ALL HOMES AND FOR children of all ages. Master a few of them, and any time you have ten minutes, you can streamline some small part of the kids' stuff.

Think inside the boxes.

Almost any clutter counselor or book will start with some variation of the "four boxes," and that's because it's a rock solid starting point for getting rid of any kind of junk. The premise is simple: Attack any stronghold of too much stuff armed with four boxes, one labeled "Keep," one "Give Away," one "Toss" and one "Still Thinking." Put everything in, say, the desk, cabinet or toy box into one of the boxes, take them to their intended destinations, and you've made some progress.

Sit the giveaways up front.

When you've amassed even a small amount of giveaway stuff and know the intended recipient, stash it in the front seat of the car to be delivered the very next time you go out. The inconvenience of moving it around will motivate you to do the errand more quickly. Avoid putting it in the trunk, or there's a danger it will just start a second life as car clutter.

Create a staging area for items to sell.

Ordinarily, if you're a newbie on dealing with kids' clutter, it's a good idea to get rid of giveaways in small, frequent trips. But if you're intending to have a sale (or you worked up the kids motivation by hinting at a bit of profit), make sure to set up a "staging area" for sale items. Choose somewhere in which they won't get swept back into the general household clutter and where they'll be ready to go when they forecast a sunny Saturday (or when the preschool or neighborhood association announces its upcoming group rummage sale). Don't put anything into the staging area that couldn't move right into a customer's shopping bag, cleaned up, or sorted out—waiting in appropriate containers. Otherwise, it becomes another "Just Thinking" area, or a way to hold on to things while seeming like you're parting with them. Best of all, when you run out of space in the staging area you'll know it's time to have the sale, or give up on the idea and put all those lovely saleable items in the grateful hands of the Goodwill store.

When you don't have time, just take 10.

Even professional organizer Debbie Lillard, who owns Space to Spare in Philadelphia, acknowledges that finding the time to cut clutter is a major issue. "Most of my clients just don't have an hour and a half available in one piece," says Debbie, who's the mother to kids ages three, six, and nine. The "10 Thing Rule" is designed for all the busy bees and for the folks who have a hard time getting started. It's for all the times when tackling a whole container—like the pantry—or category—like the kids clothes—seems like way too much. The rule means you just deal with 10 things at one time—10 books and magazines, 10 pairs of socks, 10 pieces of the artwork on the fridge, and so forth. If you still feel like working after the first 10 (or your first 10 minutes aren't up yet), try 10 more. If not, congratulate yourself on progress made and deal with 10 more pieces of clutter tomorrow.

Gently decline gifts that add to clutter.

An editor friend of mine, Katie Frankle, was visiting Knoxville from her base in Los Angeles. At the time (I know I should be embarrassed to admit), I was still trying to complete my personal collection of Teenie Beenie Bears. Katie walked me to the car after dinner and I just had to send her home with one of the little bears for her two-year-old daughter. But you know what she said? "No thanks, that's very cute but we have all the cute little toys we can deal with in the space we have in our apartment!" This is a great way to gently redirect people who love you and your kids but still want you to take something that will just add clutter to your home. It's best to be open and honest with someone rather than lie about it ("Bob's allergic to polyester fill."). The lie is bound to come back and haunt you later. If there's just no way to keep from offending someone, take the gift and do what you will with it.

When Clutter Enablers Strike

Here are two polite responses to decline a gift that will only add to clutter:

1. "That's adorable (cool, lovely) but we just don't have the space to display it properly."

2. "For our own mental health in that cluttered house, we've set a limit on how many things the kids can bring home. Would it be okay for Susie to keep it here for a special treat for our play dates?"

Purge quickly and decisively.

I review children's books, and I cheerfully pass on high-quality extras that come my way. But if they sit in the front hall in boxes, someone will inevitably move them out of sight... where they eventually join forces with other children's books, current and castoff, and school papers, and the mortgage paperwork until one fine day I spend another half hour sorting, only to have the whole process repeat itself. Don't let sorted items slip back into spaces in the house where they're no longer wanted, requiring a second round of decision-making and relocation. Another time waster is making decisions one day—"Jessica has definitely outgrown that recorder and we're going to get rid of it," but never acting on them, so the items are re-evaluated a second time, usually with a different outcome: "That recorder in with the tambourines? Hmmm, maybe Marge's kids want it!" That's why the cardinal rule is to identify discards and giveaways and relocate them in one fell swoop.

Let the stakeholder in on the decisions.

Obviously, a two-year-old can't be in charge of figuring out which clothes still fit him or whether he really needs every Disney DVD. But in general, you'll save a lot of time decluttering if the person who will have to live with the decisions is around when you're making them. Then you don't have to go through all the boxes twice, once when you're figuring things out and a second time when your son realizes his favorite stuffed animal (this week!) might be in the mix. If as parents you tend to have conflicting ideas about what stays and what goes, it makes sense to hash the decisions out while the boxes are still open, and let the parent with the more aggressive clutter-cutting style be the one to see the discards to the trash or the Salvation Army.

Give children limited veto power.

Just because you'll have the child whose possessions are in question nearby doesn't mean that she gets to keep everything she wants. That would waste time and leave you with lots of clutter. Instead, borrow from the strategies child psychologists recommend for clothes shopping, and give both parent and child a certain number of vetoes. Or, set a number of items that have to go and let the child decide—or the child can choose one thing to keep, you a second, and so on until the space is full and the rest ends up in another of the four boxes. This tactic works with two adults, too!

Call ahead.

Sure, you've got loads of great toys and books and maybe even boxes of macaroni and cheese to share, but before you try to share them with the "needy," make sure they're wanted and needed. Call around to anywhere you're considering making a drop-off, and find out what they accept, where they are, and what hours they keep. A homeless shelter, for example, might not be able to take bottles of shampoo that are already open, but the local Y might. Some food pantries can only accept cash donations and some libraries can only accept books that have had a positive review in a national publication. The widespread needs of other groups, on the other hand, might surprise you. Some Goodwill-type stores that mail overseas will take clothes that are literally rags, and some financially stable public schools still need castoff clothes and used art supplies to furnish to disadvantaged students—or for a kid to wear if he doesn't have a change of clothes and had too much fun in art class. But make sure to find out this info ahead of time, so your kids won't end up disappointed when you think you're being kind, only to discover that organization regulations prohibit your donations.

Clutter-Cutting Basics

Make a list of all the places that accept kid castoffs. Cast a wide net and you'll be sure to find a new home for everything. Here are a sampling of potential outlets to consider:

- Preschools
- Day cares
- 4-H
- Elementary schools
- School guidance counselor offices (clothes and toiletries for disadvantaged kids)
- Church mission offices
- Homeless shelters
- After-school care programs in any income range
- Church nurseries
- Local theater groups
- Art and craft teachers
- Senior centers
- Boys and Girls Clubs
- Ronald McDonald houses (where families in varying income ranges stay during their children's hospital stay).

Show kids who will get their stuff next, when you can.
You can't always visit, say, a homeless shelter to see your donations at work, but try to stop by places to which you might later make donations, like an after-school care program or the local library. Even the tiniest toddler feels good when she sees her things in use by someone else, and if you haven't donated yet, it will plant the idea that someone else might be able to use the things that are just clutter at your house. "See those kids reading with the teacher? Maybe we should bring them some of your magazines we don't use anymore. I bet they might like that."

Emphasize the pleasure of sharing.

Point out how much joy your child's donated items will bring rather than making her feel like she's somehow above the kids who will receive her castoffs. You might say, "I bet the babies at the preschool would really shake these rattles around" instead of "Let's give our used rattles to the poor babies at the preschool." Don't teach your kids to feel sorry for others; teach them to feel proud of themselves for clearing clutter and sharing with others.

Tie decluttering to a special occasion.

Half the battle of getting rid of stuff is doing it on a regular basis, before the small excesses become a major job. A great way to remember to declutter is to tie it to a special day or recurring occasion. Have your child cull toys to donate the night before each birthday party, for example, or try on clothes and give away the ones that don't fit each time report cards come out.

Drop where you shop.

Try to schedule recurring clutter drop offs on a weekly or monthly basis, tied to errands you have to do anyway. Drop newspapers for the animal shelter on your way to fill up the car at a nearby gas station, for example. That way, your kids quickly learn that taking care of clutter is an ordinary part of the schedule, something we just do without thinking about it.

Shop where you drop.
If you want your kids to see that there's pride in giving their stuff to people who could use it more than they can, take just as much pride in shopping at Goodwill and garage sales when you need something like a Crock Pot or a picture frame. That helps your children to view reusing and casting off unneeded items as something people in their circle do— sometimes they're the givers, sometimes the recipients.

Make resale value a bonus, not a reason to declutter.

Certainly, you can make a few bucks reselling your stuff, and that's a nice extra, especially for pre-teens and teens. But the money you make is never going to come up to the money you spent for your possessions in the first place. My nephew Caleb, for example, was all excited to shuck off a few of his Game Boy cartridges, painstakingly choosing even a few that he still sort of liked, until he realized that the payoff on Ebay or at the consignment store would be only a fraction of the money he'd used to buy them in the first place—which he'd worked hard to save! So mention being able to get a few bucks for old stuff only as an extra advantage, or your child might be disillusioned and less likely to want to try to sort out some giveaways the next time. The real benefit, of course, is the extra space and making way for new things and new opportunities.

Clear Thinking

Give away doubles while they're still fresh—or in fashion!

One of the hardest habits to break is thinking, "Oh, we'll get rid of those extras someday soon!" But with the possible exception of Mickey Mantle baseball cards, a giveaway becomes less valuable as time goes on. Canned vegetables and packaged staples, for example, really do expire after a while, and most anything tastes better the newer it is. If you get rid of clothes the day after your child grows out of them, a disadvantaged child (or one whose mother is a frugal thrift store shopper) will welcome the chance to wear them while they're still in fashion. A few years from now, especially with young girls' clothes, the clothes will be "have to haves," not "nice to haves." Other collectibles, toys, videos, books, and games are going to sell for more at the trade-in store, garage sale or Goodwill if they're fairly recent. So once you know you don't want them, do everyone a favor and get them quickly to someone who does.

Make clearing clutter an everyday family chore.

If you're like most families, you've got more than a couple of ten-minute sessions of decluttering ahead of you before you meet your clutter goals—more like a couple of hundred. So put clearing and organizing in a Job Jar along with all the other recurring chores, and reward it accordingly. You might even find a kid or two who would much rather sort a box in the attic every night than load the dishwasher.

Get in the habit.

Tie clutter cutting to other regular happenings at the house. For example, "We always sort one of our drawers before *Blues Clues*," or "When we take the recyclables in, we stop for ice cream on the way home."

Reward yourself.

It's nice to work toward a house that's clear and tranquil, but while you're, ahem, in progress, that state of grace may seem far off and meaningless. So make sure to reward your workers and yourself for making time to clear out clutter, at every stage along the way. Need some ideas? How about giving the kids a nickel or dime for every recyclable bottle or can they turn up at the house, like the old days of returnable soda bottles? Or, keep a list of ten-minute possibilities on the refrigerator door and have a pizza party when you've checked off twenty-five.

Choose a helper of the day.

One family I know chooses a Helper of the Day from among the three kids, every week day. They do it for cleaning, but the concept would work just as well for decluttering. The Helper is the child you call on to, for example, help you carry the discard clothes to the car or sort out the silverware drawer while you're doing the glassware cupboard. Every other child has a break. But that Helper of the Day also receives all the everyday perks—sitting up front on the way to school, choosing the TV show, getting the extra serving of dessert. However you do it, remember to reward the parents as well as the kids, to keep all of you going on this long term project until the decluttered house becomes a reward unto itself.

PART TWO

One Area at a Time

Chapter Six

CONQUER BED AND BATH CLUTTER

THE BEDROOM AND BATHROOM ARE TWO KEY PROBLEM AREAS IN TERMS of kid clutter. If it's not an unmade bed and a layer of books and toys covering your child's bedroom floor, it's a bathtub brimming with excess bath toys and a mass of moldy towels. To make your home a neat and relaxing retreat for you and your kids, try these clutter-cutting strategies.

BEDROOM BEAUTIFICATION

Give the gift of personalized bedroom decor.

Once a child's old enough to have strong preferences about how "her" bedroom looks, consider giving her the gift of new paint or floors in place of a gift that generates clutter. Let him choose the color or shop for the materials alongside you or whoever will be doing the heavy work. That's a good way to acknowledge your child's emerging independence, without overloading him with stuff he'll have to maintain and keep neat. And if it's a paint job, it's easy enough to change when your kid's preferences shift again in a few years.

Add a comforter cover for easy bed making.

Most organizing experts recommend making the bed if you're going to do just one thing to cut the visual stress in the bedroom. This is a good rule for kids or adults. A comforter's much easier than a bedspread for short arms to pull over a mattress, though, and you can make the chore even simpler if you buy an all-cotton duvet that buttons or zips over your child's comforter. "They can be pricey, but if you buy the right kind, you can do without the top sheet on your child's bed," says Cathy Steever, a mother of four and a staff manager at a mail-order company that sells all kinds of quality bedding in the Boston area.

Put shelves in the kids' closets.

The most low-maintenance way to maximize closet space is to add shelves that kids can reach. Throughout her children's younger years, Jill Williams kept a set of freestanding shelves in the bottom of her children's closets: "When kids are younger, they have so much stuff that doesn't fit in drawers, but they also don't have a lot of things to hang up," says Williams, a neatnik mother to two young teens and stepmom to two young adults in Grantham, New Hampshire. "Even if they do have clothes that could be hung up, they usually won't do it. But they will stuff those things on shelves."

Put your small things on ice.

You can keep small bedroom items like baby booties organized by storing them in an empty plastic ice tray in the dresser drawer. Baby socks, barrettes, and headbands can go in there, too.

Tackle hair stuff with a tackle box.

When your daughter's got longer hair and high hopes for fancy braids and bows, it's tough to keep track of all the little barrettes, hair bands, and hair marbles long enough to indulge her wishes, and they all seem to get jumbled up in a basket. But see if this won't do the trick: a plastic tackle box like the ones fishermen use to sort their lures. Little bands and barrettes can go in the small sections up top, larger bows and maybe even a brush in the portion below. Best of all, the whole thing snaps closed, so the doodads won't mysteriously float out or get pinched by toddler siblings.

For the preschool and kindergarten set, try cardboard drawers.

No, they may not fit in with your fancy decor like that carved walnut, but cardboard dressers are much easier for little fingers to open and shut, which makes "pick up and put away" times much less frustrating. They do come in nice patterns, or you can cover them with fancy wallpaper or just store them out of sight behind the closet door.

Plan a fashion show.

The best way to sort through girls' clothing is with a fashion show. Here's the basic approach: "invite" your daughters and any friends or relatives that share hand-me-downs to a weekend afternoon fashion show. Then get out all the clothes and try them on, putting them into "Keep," "Give Away," "Throw Away" and "Still Thinking" boxes straight from the "dressing room." When your child looks up to the girl who's passing down some clothing, it's especially good if the older child can attend and see how the clothes look on her young admirer. Make sure to serve some cookies and punch or snacks during the "show," and play music the younger set will really like.

Clear Thinking

Three old favorites you may not need.

Just because these furniture items are mainstays in children's bedroom design doesn't mean you have to use them. Clutter-wise, it may make more sense to do without these three:

Say "never" to a nightstand. Just as they are for adults, a nightstand can be a clutter magnet for kids. Who takes the time to sort through the miscellaneous drawer contents or right that stack of papers and books that's threatening to topple off the top? Instead, consider a floor lamp to place next to your child's bed and a travel coffee mug to place on the floor next to him for water.

Skip the extra bed. Twin beds have been popular since the days of Ricky and Lucy and before, but if you only have one child, you probably don't need to sacrifice extra bedroom space for a twin guest bed. Even if you're planning lots of sleepovers. Fact is, most kids are going to sleep on the floor or in the living room next to the DVD player!

A desk might be a "don't." The dream is that your child will have a beautiful, modular, well-organized study desk in his room. But don't invest in the space-hogging piece of furniture if your child actually does homework on your computer or at the dining room table. This is a good time to try before you buy, placing an old card table in the spot you hope to later fill with a fancy desk.

Manage Your Kid's Books

Any reading expert in America will tell you the importance of a child owning his own books. An entire organization, Reading Is Fundamental (RIF), is dedicated to providing kids with books. But that doesn't mean they have to overflow your kids' bedrooms! Here are a few tactics to try to keep reading levels up and clutter levels down:

1. Go with the flow—stack books on their sides. Mom Jill Williams of Grantham, New Hampshire, noticed that her kids seemed constitutionally incapable of placing books in an upright position on a bookshelf, which meant books every which way and lots of visual clutter. "I decided I might as well settle on stacks of books on their sides, since the kids were already doing that," says Williams, who maximizes the storage space lost by the stacks by spacing plastic shoeboxes or baskets in between them for other items.

2. Keep outgrown books, just not in the bedroom. Cherished stories are one thing your child will want to share with his own children, but make sure to sort through books at least once a year and put the outgrown titles away on a storage shelf. "I keep my kids' old books organized on shelves downstairs where they can get them anytime they want, but they're not taking up space in their bedroom," says Williams.

3. Use a tote bag for nightly selections. Instead of just masses of books on the nightstand or under or in the bed, have your child make selections and then put them in a tote bag next to the bed for that night's bedtime stories. In the morning or afternoon, "return" the books and choose some others. Not only does this keep the bed, floor, and bookshelf neater, it's a nice ritual for a child who may not see a parent who works outside the home until later in the day, and it sets a clear limit on how many books you'll read ("When the bag is empty, it's time for sleep.") And when it's time to move some outgrown books out of the bedroom to make room for some new ones, it's easier to make the call based on what you see your child selecting most often.

4. Check it out before you bring it in. Kids books are one of the few possessions that research shows boost both a child's self-esteem and his reading level, but you should still make sure the book will be a hit before purchasing it for the home library. The public or school library is a great first step, and lots of fancy book stores also host story hours and romping rooms where you can read a child a book before purchasing. The one exception is garage sale books—if they're age appropriate and on great sale, pick them up, but create a holding area for them at home where they stay until you decide if they're keepers or go back into a box for Goodwill.

5. Feel free to break up a set. Savvy retailers sell all sorts of books in sets these days, but scrutinize them carefully and follow the "try before you buy" strategy before committing to keeping a whole set in your child's bedroom library. With the exception of Dr. Seuss, Harry Potter and maybe the Narnia series, usually a few representative favorites in a series are better than the extensive set, particularly if you know you can access the other Spot, Berenstain Bear and American Girls books at the local library. Three key questions to consider, "Is this a book my child will want to read time and time again? Loan to others? Keep for his own children?" Make sure the answers apply not just to, say, *Anne of Green Gables*, but also all the lesser-quality sequels sold in the same set.

6. Let a pre-teen collect—but sparingly. If your pre-teen is adamant about amassing every book in a certain beloved series, like Nancy Drew or Goosebumps, that's fine, but keep it to one or at the most two series or you'll soon have the house covered with paperbacks.

7. Ignore your impulses. Instead of hitting the bookstore with credit card in hand on rainy Saturdays, browse there for an hour or two to create a "wish list" of books you want to try from the library first, or look for online or at the used book store.

Store stuffed animals off the bed.

Display them somewhere that's not disturbed every night, like a shelf, a broad windowsill, or even a board on top of two cinderblocks near the floor. That way you won't waste a lot of time putting them back in order every morning. And when it's time to get rid of a few, you'll know which ones are less important to your child because they'll be neat and tidy on the shelf, not one of the trusted few you allow to sleep with him on the bed.

Out with the old, in with the new.

Have your teen try on her entire wardrobe before a shopping trip for new clothes. This doesn't mean you'll accompany her to buy new clothes, but you can immediately give away anything that's been out-grown among the stuff she's already got. You can also veto something unsuitable just once, not every morning as she's going out the door. Here's another strategy: Agree on a certain number of outfits for her wardrobe. That way if she's not willing to part with, say, a sort of small-ish dress or '70s style outfit you're pretty sure she'll never wear, there's no conflict between the two of you—but she does have to count it as one of her allotted outfits in place of something new.

Don't let your teen keep a "goal" outfit.

Just as you shouldn't keep a too-small outfit in your closet for the time when you might lose weight, neither should your child. For one thing, it's depressing, not inspiring. For another, someone else can use that outfit right now, and by the time your child's down to the ideal weight for it, it will most likely be out of style. Better to emphasize to your daughter the dangers of growing girls' dieting.

BATHROOM BEAUTIFICATION

Make towels easier to hang.

Nothing clutters up a bathroom faster than a pile of damp towels on the floor—and they're destined to clutter the laundry room when they form mildew from the damp. You can help a child as young as two hang up a bath towel if you sew a cloth loop to each of two corners (or use iron-on Velcro to attach the loops, it's quicker). Hang two lightweight hooks on the bathroom or bedroom wall at the child's eye level, fourteen inches apart, and show him how to thread the loops over the hooks. Voila! The towel can get some air to dry and maybe be used again, and there's no chance it will slip to the floor as it might if you hang it from a standard towel rod.

Rotate tub toys.

Hard to say why it's so tempting to dump a huge pile of plastic floating toys into the tub each time your child bathes—maybe it's the splash! In any case, no child can play with every toy every evening, and the big collection is an unsightly mess between uses. Just as you might rotate ordinary play things, group four or five tub toys in each of several buckets, and just keep one set handy for bathtime, changing it up every couple of weeks or more often if your child prefers. Make sure the out-of-rotation toys are out of sight, cleaned, and dry, and they'll appear as new the next time they come out. Plus, you're much less likely to cave in to your child's requests for new tub toys when you know you've got fifteen or twenty "like new" toys in reserve already.

Keep tub toys in a dish drainer.

This helps them dry more quickly, which prevents mildew. You can easily store them out of sight by putting them in a spare drainer beneath the sink.

Double up on shower curtains.

Use twice as many hooks and attach two shower curtains side by side on one curtain rod. A luxury, yes, but they'll hang easily and always shut completely to hide that pile of kid toys and fruity soaps in the tub behind them—something you're never sure of with one standard-size curtain.

Buy just one theme bath product.

Even the mainstream supermarket sells those tantalizing bathing products with kid-theme tops. You know, the bubble bath shaped like The Little Mermaid or the shampoo that has Piglet on the top. These are great, they're fun and they should only tempt you once. After that, buy a funnel and some plain shampoo and bubble bath, and pour it into the theme container ever after. If you don't, you'll buy enough shaped containers to stock a small general store, and they'll overrun the tub, even empty.

Show expired items the exit.

Here's a great ten-minute task with dual benefits. Go through the medicine and undercounter bathroom cabinets and toss all the expired stuff, starting with the kids' sunscreen, vitamins, and, of course, prescription medicine (which should be out of reach or locked up, too). At the same time, look for giveaways among items you haven't used in six months or more, from tub cushions and kid conditioner to toilet seat covers shaped like Sponge Bob. These culls will not only cut down on clutter, they'll make the spaces you have more efficient and less likely to get messy in the process. One example: If you clear the six-year-old bath oil beads and crusty hand lotion from the medicine cabinet, you may actually have enough space to store today's toothpaste inside instead of it oozing out all over the counter.

Chapter Seven

STREAMLINE PLAY SPACES

KIDS JUST WANT TO HAVE FUN AND PARENTS ARE ALL FOR THAT—BUT DO they have to make such an awful mess when they play? Absolutely not, especially if you take some ten-minute chunks of time to rearrange play stuff storage, rotate the stock and share the excess responsibly. One extra thing is to retool your gift habits so there won't be so many toys to deal with in the first place.

Remove the toy chest.

They look great and nostalgic and all, but one big toy box encourages kids to dump everything in one big heap, and they'll spend far more time digging through it than actually getting to play with their trucks and teddy bears. Instead, try smaller containers, some of them with lids for small-piece sets, baskets, and tubs for soft, bulky toys.

Clutter-Cutting Basics

Rotate the stock.

Keep just a few things kids will enjoy out at one time, storing the others out of sight. You get three benefits that way: less visual stress, fewer overwhelming choices for young children, and toys that seem like new when you put them into the rotation. Try to stay disciplined with this approach, though, making sure to sort, clean, and mend any toys that are coming into the play room or taking a sabbatical. That way you're cutting clutter as you go, and any toys that are outgrown before their next appearance are all ready to go to younger cousins or Goodwill.

Sort by kid, sort by theme.

Judy Dunn of Maryville, Tennessee, now a grandmother and mother to three grown kids, cut down on toy clutter through the years by letting each child fill one large basket with personal play things. After that, any new toy or game had to displace an old toy or game. Even if you use more than one container, you can sort play things by child, or by theme. It's really easy to see if you have too many, say, squirt guns and water balloons when you get them altogether in one place. You can also prevent accumulating too much of any one thing by using Judy's "this much space for these toys" rule even if you're sorting by type of toy, not who owns it.

Label tubs with words or pictures.

Labels always make it easier to know where to put stuff, and depending on your child's age, the words or photos can also help them build reading vocabulary or learn shapes and colors. Cutting magazine photos for labels is a nice way for kindergarten-age kids to pass an afternoon, and of course you can pitch the magazines to cut some clutter after the project, too.

Use a dishpan to store smaller toys.
They're inexpensive, fit on shelves or can slide underneath the bed for storage—and are just the right size to house small dolls, blocks, Beanie Babies, and action figures.

One theme at a time.
"When my son Greg was younger, he organized his toys by theme— Hot Wheels, Legos, soldiers," says Jill Williams, a mother of two. "We'd store the toys in plastic tubs with lids, and it really cut down on clutter when we made the rule that he could only have one 'theme' container open at a time."

Build an instant "garage" for toy cars.

This is a great way to store Matchbox cars and a fun, quick project to do with your young son or daughter. Just grab five or six empty toilet paper rolls and a handful of small black binder clips. Stack the rolls in groups of five, three on the bottom and two on top, and fasten them front and back with the small clips. Presto change-o, each roller becomes a parking spot for a little car. Store the little garage on a shelf within reach or even right on the floor next to the play area. If you've got bigger cars, use mailing tubes and glue or wooden spring clothes pins.

Designate a "parking space" for big toys.

Use masking tape to mark off places for your kid's larger items, like baby buggies and tricycles on the floor or the carpet. That way your child will know where everything goes. If you are having particular trouble with the spot being filled with other junk the second the over-size toy is moved, have your child place an orange cone or two-liter soda bottle weighted down with sand in the spot as a place holder each time he takes the toy out.

Remove toys on a trial basis.

Because kids younger than six or seven can't always verbalize which toys they really treasure, it helps to have a grace period during which they can retrieve giveaways. "Sometimes I will set some toys they aren't using as much in a storage area for three months and see if they ask for it," says Tammy Southards, a professional organizer and mother of two boys in Green Bay, Wisconsin.

I Can Do It Myself

Kid-friendly toy containers.

Pick kid-friendly toy containers and your child can do a lot more of the sorting and putting away herself:

Picnic basket container. Raid the garage for that old wicker or wooden picnic basket—it's the perfect carryall for toddler and preschooler toys. The lid is easy for little fingers to open and close when they're picking up their toys, and the handles allow you or the kids to tote the day's play items to the living room or a play date. And for moms who get tired of plastic all the time, they're even fairly decorative.

Plastic milk jug container. Cut the spout from an empty gallon plastic milk jug and clean it and dry it. Fold duct tape over the edges around the rim and you've got an excellent (and cheap!) holder for small blocks, markers, army men and so forth. It slides nicely onto a shelf or rests firmly on the floor, and the handle makes it easy to move the collection to another room—or hold in hand as you pick up at the end of play time.

Crates with casters. This kind of container lets your child wheel his toys right over to the toy shelf, bed, or closet.

Keep off the carpet with small pieces.

If your child just loves those sets with infinitesimal doll shoes or blocks, or even if he just favors puzzles, building sets, or miniature figurines, give yourself a fighting chance to recoup all the pieces by putting a sheet down on the carpet during play time. At the end of the session, have your child pick up his things and then pull up the four corners of the sheet to shake what he's missed to the middle. This method means no tiny blocks to step on in the dark and no arguments over whether everything got put away.

Make or order a pocket curtain.

Turn a spare wall or the back of a door into premium toy storage with a pocket curtain you make by attaching bandanas or cloth napkins to a fabric curtain with fabric glue. These are particularly nice for treasured role-playing toys that your child has named and assigned personalities to, because you can tell them the soft fabric is a bed of sorts, and they can put the Barbies, Beanie Babies, or action figures to "sleep" until it's time to play again. You can also write the toy or doll's name on its pocket. If you don't have the energy to make a pocket curtain, you can also go online and order a plastic or mesh shower curtain with built-in pockets.

Put doll clothes in plastic shoe organizers.

Use the type that fits over the closet door. This kind of "see what you get" storage is also good for dress-up jewelry, small cars and toys, containers of modeling clay, and smaller action figures.

Mark your puzzle pieces.

Next time you have ten minutes, see if you can't complete one of the playroom puzzles. If it doesn't have all its pieces, consider sending it to the mixed paper recycling. If it's a particular favorite, glue a few of the most appealing pieces to a plain cardboard photo mat for a fun picture frame and then recycle the rest. If, miracle of miracles, it does have all its pieces, flip them over with your child and place a dot of water-based marker or nail polish on the back, using the same color for the back of each piece and then drawing a picture using the same color marker on the back of the puzzle box. Proceed the same way with all the puzzles you like and wish to keep, using a different color marker for each. The next time a puzzle piece appears out of nowhere, you can turn it over to the plain side to put it back in its rightful box.

Make a universal board game supply kit.

Nothing's more annoying than trying to keep track of all those little board game pieces, particularly when a crucial piece goes AWOL and you can't play. Take ten minutes to stock a resealable plastic container with everything you might need for all the board games: a set of playing pieces, a couple of timers, a deck of ordinary playing cards and small pads of papers and pens and most definitely four to six dice. If they're not of any particular sentimental value, you can then take the corresponding pieces out of each board game and get rid of them.

Make sure board games are in great shape before giving them away.

Board games your family plays regularly, or that the kids played as toddlers, are one of the few pieces of kid paraphernalia worth holding onto for the next generation. They stir so many memories and make a great heritage to share. Games that you don't use are great to pass along to a church that does Mother's Morning Out, an afterschool care program, the church nursery or a homeless shelter. But a game that's lost its pieces isn't going to do anyone any good. When you and your children are deciding on discards, figure out what you need to do to make a game complete and do it before passing it anywhere but to a recycling center. It will quickly destroy any impression you've made on your child if your family passes along stuff that is useless—or if you don't even bother to find out if it has all its pieces.

When your child's outgrown playthings, have him show someone else how to play.

Increase the value of pass-along games or toys by asking your child to donate some time with them. If your child's old enough and local chapter policies permit, have her accompany the toys and game to the donation destination and take some time to show the recipient kids how to play with them. Just a few places to consider are children's hospitals, Boys and Girls Clubs, Mothers Morning Out groups or church nurseries, homeless shelters (although they're the ones most likely to have privacy rules prohibiting children from visiting), Head Start programs or preschools, and after-school care centers. If there's not a charitable organization that makes sense, it's still a good idea to have your child teach the kids how to play, even if it's just the neighbors or his cousins. It makes him see the value of his donations and also the value of sharing his time.

Test-drive toys.

For big-ticket items that your child's just burning to try, arrange a trial period. It may cost a little extra money, but it will be worth it if you find out that a toy or game is not going to work out before you spend the big bucks—and before it's an immovable object in your family room. You can do this by renting an item or asking a friend if you can pay a little surcharge to borrow their version for a few days.

Get it at the library.

Instead of purchasing new toys or board games, see if your community library offers the opportunity to check out toys like bags of Legos and board games. Once you know you love them, maybe you'll want to buy your own, but in the meantime, the clutter goes back every time the books are due.

10 Minutes of Prevention

Help kids prioritize their wish list.

Part of the fun of toys and games is plotting, planning, and anticipation, and not necessarily because all the wishes will come true. When you're planning for holiday gift-giving, or your child's received some gift money, ask her to write down what toys she says she "has to have" on index cards, or, if the kid's old enough, have her do it herself. Then ask her to sort the cards in order of importance. That validates her wants, because you are acknowledging them, but only on index cards. Every few days, have her sort the cards again. Then choose the top three or however many seem reasonable, and apportion them out between you and whomever is bound and determined to buy your child a gift.

10 Minutes of Prevention

Three ways to cut down on the Christmas haul.
What is it about Santa and the Christmas holiday that brings
out the spirit of over-giving? Even when your child isn't
asking for too much, it often appears under the tree, from his
well-meaning parents or all those doting relatives. Try to stop
the deluge, or at least slow it a bit, with these tactics:

**If you're a practicing Christian, practice being like the Wise
Men.** Some families limit their child to three gifts at Christmas,
the amount the Wise Men brought to baby Jesus. By the
same token, the children are expected to give three gifts to
people less fortunate than they, either from the new toys
that people have given them or by refurbishing some toys
they already have and wrapping them up.

When you know others are giving big gifts, scale back yourself. If you just can't convince, for example, well-meaning grandparents that your daughter doesn't need an X-Box and her own DVD player this year, limit your own gifts to her at Christmas. Focus instead on time spent together and some rituals, or maybe a special excursion.

Ring bells for The Salvation Army during the holidays. This will help your kids be aware of people who aren't as fortunate as they are, and may make them more willing to donate some of their excess gifts to the cause after the holiday.

Let grandma share memories, not more "stuff."

A good way to let your parents and other relatives know how important they are in your lives is also a way to keep the number of big toys and excessive gifts to a minimum. On special occasions, ask those who are near and dear to your children to give them a gift of time for their birthday, not a toy. It doesn't have to be anything lavish, maybe just a walk for an ice cream treat, or a visit to the local park. Or, ask your parents to tape themselves reading a favorite book that the child already has in lieu of a gift, so your daughter can hear grandmother's loving voice as she drifts off to sleep. One more clutter-cutter that will also bring the extended family closer: Ask for a scrap book entry as a gift for your child, whether it's a written memory from an older relative, a few sketches, a favorite recipe written down that they can prepare together, or a combination of any of the above.

Chapter Eight

CARE FOR COOKING AND EATING SPACES

A FAMILY'S GOT TO EAT, RIGHT? BUT THAT DOESN'T MEAN YOU'VE GOT TO have a cluttered kitchen. Spend ten minutes at a time and you'll soon tame cluttered shelves, fridges and yes, even the dishes. You may even gain enough space to eat at the kitchen table every now and then!

Cater to your family's tendencies.

"So many people have multi-task areas that include a kitchen, living room, and dining room, and they're a natural place to come in and drop stuff that doesn't belong," says professional organizer Lynda Foxman, owner of The Organizing Group in New York City. "Instead of fighting that natural instinct, create a place for the drop-offs, maybe with hooks in the entryway or a small shelf. If the kitchen is your space for mail and paper, create a space for that, too, like a basket or a clear plastic crate."

Clutter-Cutting Basics

Fight food decay.

Food going bad in the fridge is an arch-enemy of organization—it hogs space you could be using for fresh food and makes you have to sort stuff every time you want, say, a ham sandwich. And pity the hapless kid who's moving stuff around in the fridge and accidentally spills that rancid tomato sauce. Concentrate your ten-minute efforts on moving food out once it goes bad and arranging the contents of the fridge so you can see what's what.

Keep the paper under control.

"In the kitchen, a family shouldn't need any more paper than maybe a recipe file, a calendar, and a simple pad with a pen in a drawer or attached to the refrigerator," says Debbie Lillard, the principle owner of Space to Share organization consultants in Philadelphia.

Keep your pens with your pads.

Another critical part of the simplified kitchen message system is having a pen to write with. Instead of a pencil cup, which takes up counter space, cut a pocket off an old pair of cargo pants and use fabric glue to attach it to the notebook. Voila! A pencil holder that can be stored in the drawer with the notebook.

Jot this down . . . use a simple notebook for kitchen messages.

Those cute preprinted grocery list pads that have chocolate listed as items one and two, or even Post-Its, aren't that functional in the kitchen, mostly because it's hard to write on something that's posted on the refrigerator, and the pen, even on a string, is always getting lost. And, once you tear a message off the pad, who will ever see it? Instead, take phone messages and write grocery lists and instructions for defrosting the lasagna in a plain old spiral notebook. That cuts down on paper clutter and provides a running record of family communications ("See, it says right here that I have band on Thursday!").

Clear Thinking

Plan to eat out.
Most of us shop like we'll require all fresh vegetables and lean cuts of meats for the family dinners we prepare at home every night. But reality might be far from that, and all that fresh food goes bad in the fridge while we dial out for Chinese or run the kids by the Burger Barn. Better clutter-wise to acknowledge that, yes, we do eat out, maybe pretty often, and plan a grocery list that covers only the meals you'll need to eat at home. And ironically, if you write down on the calendar precisely which nights you'll dine elsewhere (after sports practice or nights when mom works late are always potential candidates), you may find yourself eating out less. That's because when you can see that you plan to call out for pizza on Tuesday, you're much less likely to do it spontaneously Sunday or Monday, too.

I Can Do It Myself

Add a lazy Susan to your fridge.
Put kid-friendly items in reach of little hands by adding a small lazy Susan to the front of your refrigerator shelf. That way, nothing they need hides in the back to spoil or freeze and they have easy access to pudding cups, juice boxes, and anything else that strikes their fancy.

Wash bulk veggies to keep them fresh.

Retail vegetables are ordinarily covered in bacteria that speeds their decay. Fill a sink with water and a half cup of hydrogen peroxide and wash and rinse, say, the zucchini before you store it. By doing this, you can extend its life by at least a few days. This isn't necessary for prepackaged vegetables, like salad mixes or broccoli florets, that are prewashed or "ready to eat."

Buy in bulk only when it's a family staple.

Food clubs, wholesalers, and other warehouse stores that sell huge quantities of brand-name goods at very good prices market heavily to busy young families, but that doesn't mean you should do your grocery shopping there. Instead, only buy the "tried-and-true" products from them—things you know your family likes and will eat in mass quantities, like milk, bread, or pesto. If it's a food you've never tried, try a smaller quantity from another retailer first. Even though it will cost more, you won't have to waste as much if no one likes, say, the garlic pita chips or hot-pepper cheese. Not only will a warehouse-sized food experiment gone awry clutter the shelves for a long time, you can't really give large opened boxes of food to any charitable organization.

Three Shopping Tactics That Cut Down on Fridge Clutter.

1. Always purge the fridge before you shop. Take stock of what's there so you don't buy duplicates, or purchase something that has a history of going bad before someone eats it.

2. Never send a rookie to the store unless they'll follow a list. Inexperienced shoppers tend to buy the wrong brands, impulse items, and duplicates of stuff you already have, which can all clutter up the pantry or fridge.

3. Take the picky eater with you. That way, she can give thumbs up or thumbs down to food while it's still on the grocer's shelves, and you won't have it decaying in your fridge while it takes up space.

Fix up some freezer shelves.

The freezer usually has little or no shelving, so, of course, you and the children pile containers on top of each other, resulting in lost package and groceries that cascade out when someone opens the door. To give yourself a fighting chance of an organized freezer, buy some wire racks in the storage section of the discount department store and set up some compartments. If you want to experiment with the right dimensions before you commit, try upended shoeboxes, folding trays, etc.— anything that doesn't mind being frozen.

Cut back on salad dressing bottles.

No one could possibly need all the salad dressings that accumulate on the average refrigerator door. To gain some space and also stop the bottles from jumping or sliding out every time you open the door, first eliminate any dressings that have expired. Use up the others and then switch to home-made salad dressing! You can make a single bottle of it from ingredients you likely have on hand anyhow, and then vary it with some extra herbs and spices on days when you don't feel like the same old stuff. Best of all, if you get the kids involved in the mixing and the tinkering with ingredients, they'll be much more likely to develop a favorite concoction without several refuse bottles doing time in the fridge!

To make two cups of basic salad dressing: In a jar with a tight-fitting lid, mix a cup of canola or corn oil with ⅓ cup olive oil, ½ cup white wine vinegar, ½ teaspoon each salt, pepper, sugar and seasoned salt and 1 clove garlic, minced.

To vary the dressing, add one or a mixture of the following to one cup basic dressing: 1 tablespoon Dijon or grainy brown mustard; 1 teaspoon dried Mediterranean herbs such as basil, oregano, thyme or a mix; 1 tablespoon minced black olives or capers; 1 tablespoon pesto.

Clean out the fridge on trash night.

See what food needs to be pitched and immediately throw it out and then take the trash out to the curb right away. (This way, you won't have to deal with the smell of old groceries in your kitchen trash can and you'll remember to regularly purge the fridge.) Once you get in the habit, the clutter cutting gets easier and only takes but a few minutes extra time.

Eliminate expired canned foods.

If you need extra motivation to move those extra cans out of the pantry, keep in mind (and remind your kids) that even the food pantry isn't allowed to accept them once they go out of date. Look for the expiration date on the side of the label or the end of the can, and make sure to make your donations well in advance.

Use the "three-box method" to sort an entire cabinet, shelf, or area of the refrigerator.

Almost any kitchen-organizing task can be broken down into a manageable ten minutes of sorting when you've got three boxes on hand to make it easier. Just make sure you take everything out of the cabinet or off the shelf— no exceptions made for heavy punch bowls or six boxes of cereal. Then put back only what you need and will use—everything else goes into a "Give Away," "Throw Away," or "Still Thinking" box.

Clear Thinking

Give away duplicates.
It's tempting to keep, say, two pizza cutters or duplicate sets of mixing bowls. But in reality, the extra one will just take up space, and with all that clutter you'll be lucky to find one of what you need, much less the extra—give it to someone who can use it right now!

Neatly store plastic bags by stuffing them into an empty paper towel tube.

Store them in a drawer or cabinet that is easy to access.

Contain-erize your cabinet contents.

To keep little packets of sauces and those single-serve pastas and hot cereals the kids are so fond of from scattering all over the cabinet, group similar stuff and put them into small plastic containers. For food in tiny boxes, like Jello or pudding mix, use clear plastic shoeboxes you can buy at the dollar store.

Clutter-Cutting Basics

Catch up with the dishes.

When you've got a sink full of dirty dishes, the visual clutter is bad enough, but soon enough you'll have a counter full of dishes, too, followed by the kids eating cereal out of coffee mugs and so on until the whole kitchen's a mess. If you just have a few minutes for kitchen clutter each day, one of the most effective ways to spend them is on keeping the dishes loaded. At the very least, do some of the dishes every day, and though you won't overcome the clutter, it won't get worse. Along with reducing the everyday mess, if you're dealing with the dishes daily, you'll soon realize which pots, silverware, and small appliances you're using regularly, and which you could get rid of with no one missing out.

Delegate someone for dishwasher patrol.

To get your family in the regular habit of loading dishes into the dish-washer or doing dishes after each meal or snack, consider delegating the managerial duties to one of the more aggressive household members, instead of putting mom in charge and having her do the work for everyone. Amy Witsil, a mother of three teens in Chapel Hill, North Carolina, put her oldest child in charge of making sure everyone loaded the dishes after meals. "She knew if her brothers didn't load their dishes she would have to, so she made sure they stuck to it," Amy says.

Clear Thinking

Teach a young child to take care of her own dishes.
Sometimes we're so busy nurturing our young kids that we
forget they could be taking on new tasks and gaining self-
confidence in the bargain. A great job for a child once she's
four or so is keeping her own dishes clean and organized,
says organizing expert Monica Ricci, owner and founder of
Catalyst in Atlanta. "You can give even little children their
own cabinet where they can store their own plastic plates
and sippy cup, and make it a responsibility to wash them and
put them away or put them in the dishwasher and set their
places at the dinner table," she says. "Mastering small tasks
helps kids feel good about themselves."

If your kids pack lunches, it's a great idea to bunch all the preportioned foods in one box or bin.

Or just put them on one shelf. The benefits are manifold: the kids can find lunch food more easily, you know when you're out of certain items, and you can encourage young children to gradually become more responsible for rationing their own treats. Just communicate the policy that you buy lunch foods once a week and any that run out are gone, so if the kids eat up all the fruit snacks on Day One, they'll be toting peanut butter crackers for dessert the rest of the week. One other advantage is if all the "takeout" foods are in one area, you can quickly spot and pass along lunch items that no one likes.

Chapter Nine

IS THAT A CAR OR A CLUTTER MAGNET?

WHETHER YOU HAVE BABIES ON BOARD COMPLETE WITH DIAPER BAGS and strollers or you transport a soccer team several hundred miles a week, car clutter can get out of control fast. Make even short trips more pleasant with a few clutter-clearing tactics, most of them focused on keeping unnecessary stuff out of the car in the first place.

Take it all out.

Really, except for proof of insurance and the registration, most items that ride around in the car could just as easily be stored neatly somewhere in the house, leaving you and the kids more space in the vehicle and less "stuff" like newspapers and juice bottles to generate grime and attract dust. To prove this point, take ten minutes and toss every single thing out of the car and into a box except the aforementioned documents. Come back to the task the next couple of times you have ten minutes for clutter cutting and put back in the car only items that don't actually belong somewhere else or qualify as discards. You'll be amazed at how little stuff is left in the car!

Skip the in-car trash bag.

While those little 8x11-inch bags they give out at car washes and auto clubs seem nifty, they're outdated—they can't hold enough trash to be worth your while in this day of fast-food wrappings, and they promote the idea that it's okay to put trash in the car as long as it's in a bag. Instead, strive to take all the visible trash out each time you and the kids leave the car.

Find other homes for permanent trunk residents.

Clearing out the car trunk is a good project to tackle ten minutes at a time. Take everything out, put back in the spare tire and flares, and then spend ten minutes at a time reloading any things that you know you'll need every time you travel. You'll probably be left with a very roomy trunk, but save the space for real transportation needs, such as carrying casseroles to the family reunion or a Christmas tree home from the lot.

Keep the trunk locked.

Not necessarily so no one steals the jumper cables, but so the kids don't have a chance to put unauthorized junk, like wet bathing suits, inside and forget to take them out again. Make putting something in the trunk a task only undertaken with car keys in hand.

Ride shotgun, clear the clutter.

If your kids are always vying to be the one who rides up front or gets a window seat in the car, start wheeling and dealing. Whichever child gets the privilege is also in charge of making sure that any clutter from the ride, from candy wrappers to umbrellas, makes its way out of the vehicle at the end of the trip. If the responsibility makes kids not want to ride up front, just rotate the spot and its duties, maybe adding surprise extras to sweeten the pot like being the one who chooses where you stop for treats or operates the remote control garage door opener.

10 Minutes of Prevention

Five ways to combat fast-food clutter.

If you eat on the go a lot, your car may pay the price in clutter. Try these tactics to cut down on the trash:

1. If at all possible, go inside to eat. Lots of times, the line in the drive-through takes almost as much time as going in, sitting down, eating, and throwing your papers in their trash can. Plus, the kids might get a few minutes in one of those fast-food play rooms, which is more fun for them and will help counter the extra fast-food calories.

2. Request precisely the amount of condiments you will use. And then take a few extra seconds to make sure a generous fast-food worker didn't give you extras. If you take only what you'll use, you won't have to worry about throwing out the ones you find in your glove box a few weeks later.

3. Only order water for a drink. It's healthier, it doesn't stain, and it's less likely to be saved to finish later.

4. Split or skip a combo meal. It's good for your waistline, too, but regardless of whether you're watching your weight, when you're watching your car clutter you don't need a lot of extra food in your bag. So never automatically order a combination meal for everyone. Even if it costs an extra buck or two, order precisely what you and your child ordinarily eat, splitting an order of fries or halving a larger burger if it makes sense.

5. Cancel the cute box. Unless it's a rare treat for your child to eat at a fast-food restaurant, ask the person who takes your order to place the kids' meal items right in your bag, instead of one of those brightly-colored boxes that tend to hang around the car as clutter. It's always hard to throw out something with a cartoon hero all over it, even just a cardboard container, so skip the issue by leaving it at the restaurant—and save a few trees at the same time.

Place a trash can near your parking spot.

Place a giant drum garbage can lined with a bag in the garage next to the door that leads into the house, for example, or keep an attractive trash receptacle near the driveway, if that's where you disembark. Also consider a separate recycling bin near your parking space if you tend to generate a lot of soda cans, water bottles, or discarded papers while you're driving around.

Keep a tub in the car for strays.

"We're big believers in tubs," says Maryellen Duckett, a longtime soccer mom who has often logged hundreds of miles in one week transporting one of her three daughters to soccer tournaments or carpooling to school from her home in Powell, Tennessee. "I keep one of those Rubbermaid tubs in the van for stray shoes and books and so forth. That way, when someone says, 'Where is it?' they know to look there first. It also keeps loose items from falling out of the car when you're not looking." And, it's easier to carry one tub full of everything that doesn't belong in the car into the house than it is to make several little trips carrying a shoe here, coffee cup there.

Designate some toys as "ride only" playthings.

When all your son's army men are sticking out of the seat cushions and your daughter seems to bring along a different teddy bear each time you take a drive—and then leave it in the car—it may be time for a toy treat. No, not so they'll have even more toys to ride in the car, but so they'll have a couple of really tantalizing things that only come along on car rides and are off limits the rest of the time. Conversely, other toys stay in the house and don't ever come along to clutter up the vehicle. A few suggestions for the special toys include puppets, a handheld video game, Etch-a-Sketch, a plastic zipper bag full of pipe cleaners—and once the allure is gone, try something else.

For long trips, corral clutter into a cake pan.

Load a covered cake pan with crayons, coloring books and small toys
for children to take on long car, plane, or train trips. The top works as
a solid surface for drawing and the whole thing will fit neatly into a
backpack, small suitcase, or under the front seat of the car.

Buy used books and magazines for the road.

Instead of packing up hardcover books for long car trips, make a quick stop at a used bookstore and grab some comics, magazines, and deeply discounted paperbacks. That way you can leave books you're done with at the hotel or at a used bookstore or Goodwill collection box at your destination, instead of crowding the car with enough reading material for the whole trip.

Ditch the fancy in-car entertainment for audio books.

Those DVDs and televisions that hook into the car lighter are delivering better and better pictures all the time, but they take up space, as does toting along DVDs to watch. Once your kids are old enough for chapter books, try listening to books on CD in the player that's already built into the car, instead. Besides building your child's listening comprehension skills and allowing them to appreciate the passing scenery at the same time, books on tape last longer than DVDs, so you only have to bring one or two, even for trips that last more than eight hours. And unlike your favorite movies, you won't be tempted to clutter the car or recreation room with personal copies of every audio book you like, since they cost $25 and up for just one. It's much cheaper to rent and return one or two from the library, and that leaves less clutter, too. Good audio choices for the whole family include Harry Potter books, books by Lemony Snicket, Nancy Drew and Hardy Boys mysteries, and, for middle school-age kids, Phillip Pulman's Golden Compass Series and some adult mystery novels.

Take your MP3 player on the road instead of CDs.

Over-the-sun-visor CD holders are helpful, but it's even neater not to have any CDs in the car at all. One solution: If you already have an MP3 player such as an IPod and it won't break the bank, spend an extra $100 to buy a device that enables the MP3 to play over the car radio, such as IPod's RoadTrip. You can even create separate "collections" of music on the IPod that are agreeable to different combinations of family members who might be riding in the car together. Then load up the MP3 with music and even audio books and leave the other music at home. Better yet, have your teen sell the now unnecessary CDs on Ebay, Amazon.com or at a consignment store.

Chapter Ten

WHERE CLUTTER CONVENES

THE MAIN STORAGE CENTERS OF YOUR HOUSE, LIKE THE GARAGE AND THE basement, can get overwhelmingly cluttered over time. No one in their right mind would imply that you could conquer the mess in your garage, basement or attic in just ten minutes, or even ten times ten minutes. But there are some general guidelines to keep in mind to avoid adding to the clutter in those areas and to get motivated to start on several brief clutter-cutting sessions.

Sort it first, store it second.

Even if a big box of junk has to sit behind the bathroom door or in the kitchen, resist the urge to send containers of unsorted stuff to the attic, basement, or garage. Your chances of dealing with the clutter are definitely best while it's still in an accessible area. Otherwise, you'll just add time to the process (and demotivate yourself or your kids) if you have to locate a box in the attic and lug it to a sorting area before you can even start separating the keepers from the giveaways.

Clear Thinking

Allot space in the attic, too.

It's all too easy to think of the attic as a catch-all, a place to banish the stuff you don't really know what to do with. But it gets really cluttered really fast with that mentality. Instead, allocate space there just like you do everywhere else in the house. Just because it's out of sight, for example, doesn't mean Child A can keep thirty-five stuffed animals for posterity while Child B has a shoebox, nor that reams of unused fabric should supplant a dozen hand-embroidered dresses with sentimental value. Just as you might limit a child to a laundry basket full of "active" toys, consider putting space limits on the toys, games or clothes that go into the attic, either categorized by type or by child (i.e., "outgrown board games" or "Bill's collectibles.") Then when your son (or your husband, for that matter) has exhausted his storage space, it's time to make some decisions about giving things away.

Put specific labels on everything.

One of the best investments for "major-storage-area" clutter is a thick
black indelible marker. That way you can label all the boxes and even
plastic tubs that make it into storage with specific instructions. Examples: "Mindy's clothes, size 6, ballerina phase, to keep for grandkids"
or "George's Star Wars figures, 3 Chewbaccas included, appraised on
7/3/08 for $125." This approach makes it easier to find what you want
and also makes it so you don't have to spend a lot of time rethinking
what you've saved.

10 Minutes of Prevention

Make your attic or basement child-friendly.

The most positive step you can take to keep an attic or basement organized is to make it safe for most anyone in the family to get there and back, maybe even carrying some storage items on the way. So call a contractor and see about installing handrails, safe steps, and a door that opens and closes easily in the basement and attic. If you know children eight and up will be safe, you're much less likely to make these all-important storage spaces the domain of the adults, who may or may not have time to schlep stuff in or out. Besides, it's hard to teach your child that storing and maintaining her possessions is her responsibility when she can't readily access the ones that end up in the major storage areas.

Make an attic play space.

With a little throw rug, a file drawer, some snacks and a lamp, your school-age child could have a nice little retreat in the attic. And while that may seem like an invitation to clutter, it will actually help you keep stored items under control because at least one little soul in the household will probably regularly browse the contents of the attic.

Store boxes on pallets in the garage or basement.

That way, if the place gets damp or leaky or you have spills of fluids stored there, the boxes won't get soaked or mildewed. Pallets are widely available at the loading dock for most retailers or at home building supply stores.

Four Ways to Tie Storage Duties to the Calendar

The old adage "out of sight, out of mind" is never so true as with stuff stored in the basement, garage or attic. If you can get in the habit of examining the things stored there on a regular basis, you'll be much more likely to use the space to store needed items. Here are just a few ideas to get you started:

1. Reconsider all stored holiday and party items (for occasions year 'round) the day after Thanksgiving, before you put the tree up.

2. Look through stored letters, photo albums, and scrapbooks on the day you remember loved ones: Valentine's Day.

3. Sort through boxes of games and toys on your child's birthday or the day before.

4. Seek out recyclable items and old paint, lawn and car hazardous waste that needs to be disposed of on Earth Day in April or on the first day of spring.

Four Ways to Gain Space in the Garage

Wade Slate is father of three, stepfather to two and a full-time lawn-care professional who works from his garage and driveway in Knoxville, Tennessee. He knows how to maximize storage in the garage, and pitfalls to avoid, including the following:

Add some high shelves. Take advantage of the space over your head. "That's a great place to store things you don't use that often, like the kids' snow cone maker or the bowling bags," he says. "You just have to be sure you have a safe, sturdy stepladder to get the things back down again, and I wouldn't store anything there that a kid needs to get to often, or they're going to try to get up there without an adult."

Hang extra posters on the back of the door. Use the space on the back of your garage door or the door leading to the house to store excess wall art. "I've bought several poster frames and I keep several posters in each one, layered on top of each other," says Wade. "I'm not doing anything else with the space on the back of the garage door, so I put the poster frames up there. It's a good place for all those posters you get on vacation or at concerts and oversize kids artwork, until you decide you want to put them up somewhere better or get rid of them."

Make a makeshift storage spot in the garage rafters. Slide a large piece of plywood over the rafters and you've got instant storage for bulky, awkward items that you don't use all that often, like lawn chairs, dart boards or inflatable rafts. Don't put anything real heavy up there, though, says Wade, or it's too hard to get down again.

Attach hooks to cabinet doors. Wade also recommends putting storage hooks on the outsides of cabinet doors to hang miscellaneous garage itiems such as stop watches, Frisbees, and bike helmets. Choose a cabinet door that you don't have to open and close a lot.

Separate the garage into functions.

You'll never get a leg up on garage storage if your kids' stuff is mixed in with the exercise equipment, lawn mower, and all the other car supplies that make their home in the garage. Even if you're only chipping away at the task ten minutes at a time, make sure to start putting the kids stuff in one area of the garage, grouping "like with like" as all the organization experts recommend. That makes it easier to evaluate the fate of the items you're trying to organize and also easier to hold older kids accountable for keeping it neat.

Chapter Eleven

CLUTTER AND THE GREAT OUTDOORS

IF YOU'RE LUCKY ENOUGH TO HAVE A YARD OR AT LEAST A DECK AND SOME grass, you're probably also blessed with some outdoor clutter. Here are some ways to keep all the areas your children traverse near the house a bit more organized, along with tactics for stuff you take along when you venture into the mountains or the wide open spaces.

Don't duplicate kiddie furniture.

If you already have a cute set of table and chairs for the kids that lives inside, don't give into the temptation to buy more kid-size stuff for outside, even if the latter is made of wicker or canvas and is shaped like lawn chairs. Little kids are really quite comfortable on plastic benches and chairs, and if you just move the indoor furniture outside for play dates, picnics, and messy projects, you'll save money and space and double your chances of cleaning up afterwards, since you'll need the furniture back inside.

10 Minutes of Prevention

Buy water-resistant kid shoes.

To avoid the pile-up of muddy shoes on the porch, buy each child a pair of water or Frog shoes. Kids can take them off outside when they're muddy and rinse and dry both the shoes and their feet. Nor will you have to contend with dirty wet socks and shoes that take three days to dry out, or leave them in an ugly stack that one of the dogs almost inevitably carries off.

Make clear paths to outdoor storage and trash areas.

To cut down on items being left in the yard or on the porch, make sure the paths to outdoor storage are kid-operable and have proper drainage. Consider all the little errands kids need to run in the area surrounding the house, and have gravel or stepping stones in place so the kids can easily make their way to the trash, recycling bins, shed, bike rack, bird feeders, and so forth. In preparation for winter weather, make sure to salt or shovel those paths first.

Create a check-out system for outdoor items.

You know how the skating rink makes you leave your shoes in the cubby where you remove your rental skates? Borrow that concept for all the outdoor items that tend to get left outside. Create an outdoor or garage cubby for such items as bicycle helmets, sidewalk chalk, baseball gloves, and so forth. Then have your kids relinquish something they'll need back immediately before they "check out" a piece of outdoor equipment. It could be a ball cap, a walkman, a cold drink—anything that will trigger them to remember to put the borrowed item back in storage so they can have the other item back. To really make the system work, particularly in the beginning, leave candy or a dollar bill in the cubby every now and then as a reward for bringing the item back to its proper place.

Mount a mailbox for the kids' gardening supplies.

Don't discourage your little green thumb from working in the garden with you, but do encourage her to keep her tools in good repair and store seeds and soil properly with her own little storage space. The best option is a mailbox, used or new, mounted on a post at her eye level. It will keep everything from a tiny trowel and garden gloves to sunflower seeds and a small bag of vermiculite dry and at the ready for the next gardening activity. If you like, mount another a little higher for Mom or Dad!

Clear Thinking

Camp in the backyard to cut down on camp equipment clutter.

The biggest enemy to organized camping supplies is inertia. The stuff you rarely use tends to be the stuff that deteriorates and is inoperable when you do need it, or can't be found and then you end up with several, say, plastic egg containers or tarps. Ironically, it's better for clutter if you haul out the camping equipment once a month or so, even if you only use it in the backyard. That way you're more likely to know what you have and avoid purchasing duplicates, to make little repairs before they become big problems and to know immediately when someone's outgrown a crucial piece of equipment, like a sleeping bag, so you can replace it and give it away. You'll also learn quite quickly which supplies aren't that helpful for camping, so you can give them to Goodwill before the next trip that requires hauling them great distances. And the little adventures in the backyard are a perfect training ground for camping skills, including the ones required to stay organized.

Keep camping supplies packed.

If your family likes to camp, or you've even tried it once and would like to again, it's best to keep any "camping only" supplies ready to go. "Pack up anything you'd need on a trip that you can leave stored and generally do not need at other times—flashlights, bungie cords, tent," says Matt Witsil, a Scout leader for Troop 835 in Chapel Hill, North Carolina. That keeps camping supplies from sneaking into other areas of the house and it also makes it simpler to take people up on last-minute camping invitations.

PART THREE

Outside Interests
(and the Stuff They Spawn)

Chapter Twelve

KEEP THE MEMORIES, LOSE THE CLUTTER

KEEPSAKES AND PHOTOGRAPHS TEST THE RESOLVE OF EVEN THE MOST devoted clutter cutter. The average person is at a loss to discard anything that preserves the memory of a loved one, but there are ways to hold on to the fond memories without keeping every scrap from your family's shared history. Here are a few sensible, sensitive, and sentimental suggestions.

Keep part, not the whole.

When you're sorting inherited possessions or great collections from your immediate family, remember that you don't have to keep the whole thing to remember that period of your shared history or someone who predeceased you. Instead, consider keeping just a cup and saucer from a set of china if you won't use the whole thing and it will be a headache to store. Or choose five or six of your daughter's favorite Beanie Babies or a few favorite dolls to hold on to, instead of wrangling with the whole set. Your goal is to hold onto things that will inspire recollections in the years to come, and you only need a few representative objects for that.

Quilt 'em up.

If your memories are tied up with clothes, blankets or embroidered pillowcases, consider cutting some up for a memory quilt and donating the rest of the fabric to a local quilter's guild. The quilt is a lot easier to store or exhibit than the clothing and the quilters will probably appreciate any vintage material, particularly if it's all cotton.

Clutter-Cutting Basics

Three sensible strategies for sorting memory materials

Judy Dunn is a mother and grandmother in Maryville, Tennessee, who has taken on the tough task of sorting through the estates of several older relatives. The experiences have taught her several basic strategies for keeping some memories and still being able to toss or donate lots of "stuff," many of which hold true for other types of clutter cutting, too:

Save what was important enough for someone else to save.
"In deciding what to keep from my mother's things, I came across a letter that my grandfather had written to my grandmother. He was not a high school graduate and this was written on a scrap of notebook paper, and nothing was spelled correctly. But I saved it, because it was so important to my mother and to her mother."

Don't choose what to keep based on monetary value. "You can't know what will be valuable fifty years from now, and you can't second guess or play that game," says Judy. Instead, keep a few things that will remind you of the one you love, whether that's a favorite book you read together, a sugar bowl she kept on the dinner table or a clay figurine your daughter made in kindergarten.

Save what you think your kids would want for their own kids. "It's tempting, but you can't hang onto everything they ever brought home," says Judy, who has three adult children. "Instead, keep a few things you think they might want to show or use for their own kids, like a really nice piece of artwork or a favorite knit sweater."

Four Feel-Good Ways to Use Duplicate Photos

Unless you only started taking photos in the digital era, you probably have a good many duplicate prints and less-than-ideal photos hanging around the house. Take care of the clutter without feeling like you're wasting valuable photos with one of these suggestions:

1. Next time the class requests magazines for collage projects, send some photos, too. All they're looking for is images for the kids to cut out and all you're looking for is to get rid of some clutter!

2. If your child's an appropriate age, use the photos to make an "ABC" album or even a notebook with different letters represented by different cutouts from your photos. Remember, people's names are a great way to remember the sound of a certain letter!

3. During the winter holidays, spend some time with your preschool kids cutting out faces of family members from duplicate photos. Then glue or paste them on gift tags or right on the gifts so non-readers know who can look forward to which present.

4. Cut out faces from photos that feature more distant members of the family and paste them into a small notebook (like a memo pad) so your child can get to know family members by sight. This is especially fun before a big family reunion or wedding.

For digital photo backlog, consider an LCD digital picture frame.

With a picture frame that can rest in the living room or wherever you like and exhibit digital photos album-style, you don't have to worry about printing out digital photos or accumulating a mess of them on your computer or digital camera card. They're more expensive than a traditional photo album, but save oodles on printouts and clutter. And setting up the digital picture frame, editing the selections included on it, and discarding unwanted digital images is a great job to assign to a tech-savvy teenager who might scoff at more traditional clutter-cutting chores.

Clear Thinking

Organize jumbled photos by theme, event, or person.

It's daunting to try to get all the photos in exact chronological order, but even young children can help group photos based on who's in them or what's happening at the time. Use the path of least resistance to keep your clutter cutting moving forward.

Mail double prints right away.

If you pre-address an envelope for the photos and attach the proper postage, you can mail the photos off as soon as they're in your hand, even on your way home from the 1-hour photo store, says Pam Hix, who with Louise Kurzeka owns Everything's Together, an organizing business in the Minneapolis area. Don't risk having them sit around if you don't have a big or sturdy enough envelope at home. Just buy a 3-pack of sturdy manila envelopes when you pick up your photos at the drug store.

Chapter Thirteen

GET CRAFTY WITH
ARTS AND CRAFTS STORAGE

O F COURSE WE ALL WANT OUR KIDS TO BE CREATIVE, BUT DO ARTS AND
crafts have to clutter up the whole house? Absolutely not, if you
employ some creative strategies of your own, from keeping supplies
corralled to eating up some of the projects!

Make your own craft supply center.

Instead of forking over the cash for one of those fancy plastic carousels that holds art supplies (and usually comes with its own versions of things you already have), make a personalized version to house what you use most often. A large plastic houseplant saucer can serve as the easy-wipe base, with empty jars and frozen orange juice cans serving as the holders for paintbrushes, scissors, pens, and pencils, you name it. If you've got one to spare, place the saucer on top of a lazy Susan so kids can twirl it to reach the supply they want. The whole thing can go in a cabinet when you're not using it, if you've got the space.

Don't buy supplies to "grow into."

Whether it's knitting needles and yarn or a lavish oil paint set, don't stockpile future project supplies for your kids if they haven't learned a craft yet. Unless you live far from a discount department store, there will be plenty of time to buy what you need the day before, say, Aunt Lily is going to show your fourth grader how to crochet. You may spend a few more dollars buying supplies at the last minute, but you'll more than make up for it in space saved—and in not having to give away craft materials no one ever got interested in learning how to use.

Every picture tells a story—about where to put craft supplies.

"I have kids keep all the craft supplies in clear plastic shoe boxes," says Sharon Irvin of Bakersfield, California. A former day care center operator and professional clown, she now works at a craft supply store. "We tape a picture on the front to indicate what goes in that box, or tape the object itself to the box. That way, the kids know the popsicle sticks go in the box with the popsicle stick taped to the front. It's so easy for clean up and pick up."

Sort into see-through plastic pocket shoe holders.

Craft supplies like buttons, pipe cleaners, crayons, and beads can also go into hanging shoe bags with clear pockets, as long as you hang them low enough on a door so that your older child can reach them. Make sure they aren't choking hazards for little ones. If you like, use hot glue to attach a sample of what's inside the pocket to the front.

Start sorting chores early.

Irvin, who has four children of her own ages three to fifteen, has kids start sorting supplies with the picture/sample method as early as age two or three. "It's all part of matching and learning shapes," she says. "And it's also important that from an early age they're in charge of their own things, that they learn organization as they're growing up."

Store paintbrushes in potato chip tins.

Have any leftover Pringles containers? They're perfect for storing paint-brushes, brush side up. Cover the outside with white paper with a picture of—what else?—paint brushes attached or drawn on.

Store rolls of art supplies on paper towel or toilet paper holders.

Attach a paper towel holder or toilet paper dispenser to the door of a craft closet or the art room wall. Then use it to store spools of ribbon and rolls of masking, cellophane, and duct tape. If you need to, cut the center from the ribbon spools so they'll fit.

Use a plastic dish drainer to store coloring supplies.

Use the plate slats to hold coloring books neatly upright. If it has a silverware section, use that to hold crayons, pencils, scissors, and rulers.

Draw on expendable items.

If you've got an enthusiastic artist at the house, unleash her on decorating paper items you plan to use and toss later. Just a few suggestions include paper cups, the tops of memo pads, the fronts or backs of paper placemats or coasters, place cards for special dinners, the backs of envelopes you mail bills in, and the backs of legal pads.

Clear Thinking

Treat art as a process, not just an end product.
When it's your child's creation, it's hard to relegate it to the trash bin after a time, but you simply can't keep every bit of art or the whole house will be overwhelmed. Instead, try to instill the attitude that, "We try to make all our stuff look great, even the things we're only going to use once and then recycle. Art is about creating, but not always keeping." This mentality frees your child to experiment and have fun with art and it keeps you from feeling guilty when it's time to get rid of creative efforts. Just don't be surprised when your kid catches on to the concept much more quickly than his sentimental parent!

Use biodegradable craft supplies.

It's a lot of fun to make necklaces and mosaics with dried seeds and beans, macaroni, pine cones, dried flowers and such, but there's even more fun to be had. When the project's worn out its welcome, you and your child can make a ceremony of putting it in the compost to help the plants grow.

Make crafts with edible beads.

Most dollar stores sell candy beads. Save up your quotient of sweet treats and make candy necklaces instead of plastic or paper ones. There's no clutter when you can eat the fruits of your labor!

Decorate cookies instead of paper.

Starting as early as preschool, a cookie, some icing, and sprinkles can provide an art canvas for a child—and then, of course, he also gets the pleasure of eating or bestowing his creation. In later years, encourage teens to make up cookie bouquets for special occasions or "no reason at all" gifts for neighborhood shut-ins, or bake a batch of gingerbread men any time of year. It's art, but you don't have to worry about keeping it around or sneaking it out to the garbage in the dead of night.

Try less traditional "eat-as-you-go" crafts.

When you're considering kid craft projects that can be consumed at clean-up, expand your repertoire to include decorated salads, breakfast plates, raw vegetable platters, and the like. One favorite: Make an edible mouse sculpture from an overturned canned pear half with almond-slice ears, raisin eyes, and maraschino cherry nose. Other creative outlets that provide nutritious food include dying eggs for occasions other than Easter (in autumn colors, for example, or in school colors for big game celebrations) and shaped pancakes decorated with dried fruit and radishes cut to look like roses (they'll open up in ice water).

Have an easy-to-clean art fest in the tub.

Finger paint is a childhood experience not to be missed, but let's face it, there's really no reason to keep around most of the resulting art, and it tends to be bulky. Instead of generating clutter you'll have to reluctantly part with later, try "disappearing" finger paintings in the tub. Make the "paint" by dissolving two envelopes of unflavored instant gelatin in ½ cup hot water and letting it sit for 10 minutes. Then combine a cup of cornstarch with ⅓ cup of granulated sugar and 3 cups of cold water, stirring it in a saucepan until smooth (the cornstarch still won't be clear). Cook the mixture over medium-high heat, stirring occasionally, until it thickens, then cut the heat to low, add the gelatin mixture and ½ cup Ivory liquid, stirring until smooth and then cooling. Divide the mixture into empty plastic tubs from margarine or yogurt, coloring each one with a few drops of food coloring. Test a little on the side of your tub, making sure it will rinse off with warm water and maybe a little scouring powder. Then let the kids use what they want to finger paint the tub, rinsing the art off at the end of the adventure and storing the rest of the finger paint in airtight jars.

Shred and recycle paper art.

It's mighty tempting to spirit old paper art out in the night while your child's asleep, but a better approach is to let her shred it herself as long as it contains only water-based paint or crayons. Then, if you have trees or a garden, apply the paper shreds as mulch, beneath the pine needles or pine bark mulch if you're picky about appearances. The ritual reinforces the message that art can be permanent or a temporary thing—and that our supplies can go back into the world's resources to have a second life. If you don't have use for paper shred mulch, make sure you know where to drop off mixed paper for recycling in your area, and make sure your child comes with you to see where her stuff's going to do some more good.

Store prized pieces in a pizza box portfolio.

Go through your child's art pieces, with him or by yourself, and choose which ones are discards and which ones to keep. For the keepers, ask for an unused pizza box at your local pizza parlor (or ask the delivery guy to bring one next time you call in). It can house oversize art from school and still slip under a bed or on top of tall bookcases with ease. If you like, save even more space by gluing some of the art on the covers and sides.

Use partitioned liquor boxes to store rolled art.
You can corral everything from super science posters to school project family trees in a liquor box, as long as you can roll it up. If you're wrangling with something wider or longer, like a poster, cut the bottom off an identical liquor box and tape it to the first.

Rotate displayed child art when you change the calendar.
Judy Dunn is a mother and grandmother in Maryville, Tennessee, who
heartily recommends rotating the art on the refrigerator at least once
every four weeks. "When my three children were growing up, once a
month or so I would put something special of theirs on the refrigerator.
For my two kids who were very artistic, that would probably be a piece
of art from school, while for my other son it was usually an excellent
school paper. But I'd always replace it with something else within a
month, and that's what they came to expect so it was never a shock."

Apply the frame rule for old art.

Dunn's rule of thumb for keeping art longer than a month is, "Is it good enough to frame?" She did save and frame several fine pieces from the growing up years for her two accomplished artist offspring, but far more pieces found their way to the recycling bin. "You just can't keep everything," she says.

Chapter Fourteen

MAKE A GAME PLAN FOR YOUR SPORTS GEAR

WHETHER YOU'RE A "BIKE RIDES AFTER DINNER" KIND OF FAMILY OR YOU are harboring legions of competitive athletes, sports gear can take a toll on household organization. To stem the tide of balls, bats, helmets and such, find racks and bins that work for you and make sure to give away outgrown equipment immediately.

Always try before you buy.

Whether you rent ice skates or Rollerblades at a rink first or raid the local recreation center to experiment with a football before purchasing, make sure you know what you're getting into before buying any sports equipment for your child. A good rule of thumb is to give kids three trials somewhere else before you opt to buy, say, skateboards or tennis rackets for them.

10 Minutes of Prevention

Wait for the first team meeting to purchase team supplies.

Even if Junior is super excited about the start of PeeWee baseball, resist the urge to buy his sports supplies until you've met with the coach (or until the league gives out a detailed list of requirements). You'd be amazed at how specific the demands for even a noncompetitive league will be, right down to the color of socks. Who knew there were different-size soccer balls for different ages, for example? You don't want to end up with extras before the season even starts.

Invest in sporting equipment upkeep.

Aside from the sports stuff your kids have lost interest in and the things they never picked up in the first place, the third most common sports clutter is stuff that won't work. If you're going to own, say, a basketball or dirt bikes, make sure you research what you'll need to keep the equipment in working order, and purchase those things, whether it's an air pump, wrench sets, or mink oil, at the same time as the equipment. Remember to work the price into your total budget before deciding to buy.

Weigh in with officials to keep uniforms the same.

If your child's participating in a league, at the end of every season make sure to contact the league administrators to request that they stick with the same league uniforms. Make the same request of any coach at the end of one season and the beginning of another, if they're the ones who determine what your child will be wearing on the field or in the pool. A lot of times the people in charge will get enthused about some new line of uniforms, forgetting that individual families will have to allot more dollars—and space—for the shift. Sure, your kid will probably outgrow his uniform before next year, but if the league changes costume, you also cancel your chance to pass his uniform down to a younger child or buy used from someone who's moving up, too.

Clear Thinking

Three alternatives to the team trophy.

It's become commonplace to give little competitors a partici-
pation trophy at the end-of-season banquet. While this is
heartwarming the first time your child plays, after a few
years you end up with lots of bulky, shiny trophies that are
hard to store and take up lots of space on shelves. Instead,
offer to organize one of the following for an end-of-season
acknowledgement:

1. An Olympic-style medal, complete with ribbon
2. A T-shirt the child can wear to practice
3. A patch or pin each player can attach to his workout bag

Make a swap meet part of any season.

Don't be shy! The second the parents meet for the season, request or organize a swap meet so that families can sell or exchange outgrown equipment for that particular sport, be it flippers and kickboards, shin pads and cleats, or small-fry size basketballs. Everyone will thank you, and getting rid of the stuff your child can't use anymore right away will save you from all the sorting and charitable donation research you'd have to do if you wait a few years.

Buy a sports equipment caddy.

As always, you need to sort through what you have and discard and give away before buying anything fancy. But after that, look into the Stacks and Stacks store online or the Rubbermaid sports storage bin and see if the things you have might be contained handily in one of them. The next step, of course, is making the caddy accessible to the kids so that they slowly learn to be responsible for their own equipment. Don't put it in the garage, for example, if you tend to lock it up all the time, and ensure that there's enough space around it so kids can reach to stow their stuff.

Store sports bags near the washer.

There's really no reason why your child's cleats and jersey should clutter up her room (or release those delightful odors there). It makes much more sense clutter-wise to just keep the bag near the cleaning source, says Brooks Clark, a long-time volunteer coach and team manager for various soccer and basketball teams in Knoxville, Tennessee. "We keep all the soccer uniforms in the basement with their bags—where the washing machines are," he says.

Chapter Fifteen

KEEP HOBBIES FROM HOGGING YOUR SPACE

W HETHER YOUR LITTLE ONE PURSUES STAMP COLLECTING OR MOM HAS a kid-oriented hobby like knitting baby clothes, the incidentals from a free-time pursuit can suck up space. Make purchases sensibly, pare your supplies back to a reasonable level and neaten up the rest to keep your hobby as fun as it can be!

Sort and discard before you buy more.

One of the biggest enemies to a neat hobby space is duplicate items and unfinished projects, whether it's woodworking, quilting, or Legos. Make you and your child's next hobby "project" sorting through what you already have on hand. Naturally, that's going to take more than ten minutes, so schedule several short sessions and come armed with the four containers for stuff you want to "Keep," "Toss," "Give Away," or "Still Think About." Set up some sort of goal and reward to ease the process, whether it's ice cream after half the tubs are sorted or a brand-new craft table once you've gotten all the yarn and fabric figured out.

Organize fabrics by color and type.

Whether your daughter sews tote bags or you regularly run up costumes for school presentations, keep fabric sorted by color and type in stackable plastic shoeboxes. Felts in one bin, for example, and denims in another. Jill Williams, an avid quilter and experienced mom, found this technique to be pretty useful: "If you get the fabric organized and stored in clear plastic, you can see what's in them and plan what you need for projects," she says. "I keep the fabrics I use most often right in the work room, and put the craft fabric I use less often, like to make Halloween costumes, on a shelf down in the basement." This also provides younger kids with a great way to learn colors and appreciate textures—and maybe to get an interest in learning to sew. Williams uses plastic shoe boxes with lids, but not the airtight, Tupperware kind since fabric sealed in air-tight containers or even resealable plastic bags can mold if any moisture gets trapped inside.

Five Places to Send Hobby Extras

If you've got extra material, wood, or paints left over from your last project, seek out volunteer groups in need of the extras and make sure your child understands where the supplies are going and how this group helps. With any luck at all, your efforts will encourage your child not just to donate, but maybe to participate in volunteer efforts when she's older. Here are some places to donate hobby extras:

1. Senior citizen centers often offer painting, knitting, or quilting lessons and supplies can be expensive. See if extra oils, brushes, yarn, or fabric swatches might be appreciated.

2. Local painting, quilting, and sewing guilds usually have at least one charity project going. See if your extras might be beneficial to their plans.

3. If you live in an area with 4-H, the kids themselves are always working on charitable projects, like sewing beds for shelter dogs, and they might welcome not just castoff materials but your child's skills, too.

4. Nice scrap wood and other woodworking extras might be used by local Scouts for birdhouses and other projects.

5. Lots of churches, locally and nationally, make quilts, caps, and clothes for the less fortunate of the world. One group is Lutheran World Aid. Check your local library to research others in your area.

Roll your yarn.

One of the best ways to keep knitting clutter at bay is to roll skeins of yarn into balls right after you purchase them, says Frances Hall, a fourteen-year-old hobby knitter in Knoxville, Tennessee. "That way they won't get knotted before you can use them, and it's a lot easier to get them back in order if one of the pets discovers how much fun it is to mess around with yarn."

Keep a lid on strings and yarn.

Keep snarls to a minimum on hobby yarn by putting a ball inside a coffee can with a plastic lid. Cut an "X" across the lid with a craft knife and thread the end of the yarn through it when you're ready to work. In the meantime, though, the yarn is protected from pets and dust and can be stacked on a shelf—and you or your novice knitter are much more likely to remember to use it instead of buying new stuff since you've already invested so much effort.

Look in the hardware aisle for collectibles storage.

Those sets of small plastic drawers intended for nuts, bolts and the like in a workroom can really come in handy for other collections, says Jill Williams, a mom to two young teens and stepmom to two young adults in Grantham, New Hampshire. "A guy can use the drawers to store individual plastic figurines," she says. "They're also good to house stamps, fossils and rocks, trading cards—you name it. Best of all, when your kid outgrows the hobby, she can still use the drawer set for other things. The little drawers are deep enough for a lipstick or mascara."

Leave the credit card at home.

If you and your child are really into scrapbooking, say, or model trains, make the visit to a supplier's shop its own reward, especially if you go there often. Spend one trip browsing, chatting, and dreaming, then come back a second time to make any absolutely necessary purchases. That way you'll still have the enjoyment of being around the collectibles or supplies you love without buying a bunch of stuff you don't need— or don't need yet.

Help your kid enjoy a hobby for a time, then let it go.

Matt Witsil of Chapel Hill, North Carolina, is a father of three teens who have always been active in music, sports, Scouts, and collecting. His oldest son is particularly interested in small furry creatures and took diligent care of pet gerbils for several years. When the last one died at the ripe old age of three, Tucker was ready to stop. Instead of mourning the end of an era, letting the hobby supplies linger, or encouraging one of the other kids to pick up where Tucker left off, Matt harped on the idea, "I'm really glad we did that. That was really fun!" Then the family sold the used cage and all the supplies, with the attitude that someone else could really enjoy them and save some of the start-up costs.

Hang on to music—but neatly!

A child who's a piano student can probably pass Book 1 to another child starting out, but you really should save any of the pieces assigned to him personally by the teacher. "It's really fun to go back and play that old music again for relaxation," says Susan Crawford, who majored in music in college and occasionally substitutes on piano at her church in Knoxville, Tennessee. But the sheets aren't sacred! Susan recommends punching holes in them to store in a three-ring binder, on a shelf some-where near the piano.

Use classified ads to shed hobby extras.

Half-used bottles of essential oils from a potpourri period, first year piano books, a box of inks from calligraphy—all are things you should probably get rid of, but none of them are potentially big money makers. Instead, why not let someone else have them for free and promote a life skill for your youngster at the same time? Most newspapers have a classified ad section for "freebies." If that's available in your area, appoint a child who's nine or older to place your ads, working with her the first time to call the paper and write the description and so forth. Be sure to say in the copy if you have all the components for an unfinished project, like a model ship or cross-stitch pillow. Of course an adult will have to handle the visitors who come to pick up the supplies, but the child can give out basic information over the phone to callers, as long as she understands never to give out the home address (and if that's the only worthwhile lesson she learns from the experience, it will be time well spent!)

ACKNOWLEDGEMENTS

I would like to thank all the people who fueled these clutter-cutting ideas with enthusiasm and utter disregard for their own schedules or fame. Monica Ricci, who lives and breathes to help people realize the benefits of an organized life, was particularly helpful with summary phrases, the sisters Jill Williams and Susan Crawford were there with a smiling voice and great advice when I needed them, as was Brooks Clark, who took a break from vacation to help me. I must also acknowledge my sister Amy Witsil and her husband Matt, who never groan audibly when I need to tap yet another pocket of their bizarre and wonderful household knowledge, and Ellen Phillips, who keeps thinking of me for these fun assignments. And I am forever in the debt of editor Aimee Chase, without whose uncommon mix of cheerleading, calm, and consideration there is no book.

ABOUT THE AUTHOR

Rose R. Kennedy is the author of the *Family Fitness Fun Book* and has contributed to numerous tip books, including *10-Minute Housekeeping, 1,001 Old-Time Household Hints, Cut the Clutter and Stow the Stuff,* and *Shameless Shortcuts.* An avid food writer and kids' book reviewer, she regularly contributes to *Disney Adventures,* fineliving.com, and *The Herb Companion.* Rose lives in a nicely blended family in Knoxville, Tennessee, where she's on the board for the local Actors Co-op and is a devoted pet owner, backyard bird watcher, and NTN trivia player.

Other books in the "10-Minute" series available from Fair Winds Press

10-Minute Clutter Control
By Skye Alexander
ISBN: 1-59233-068-1
$12.00

10-Minute Feng Shui
By Skye Alexander
ISBN: 1-931421-88-X
$12.00

10-Minute Housekeeping
By Rose R. Kennedy
ISBN: 1-59233-177-7
$12.00

10-Minute Organizing
By Sara Lavieri Hunter
ISBN: 1-59233-181-5
$12.00

10-Minute Home Repairs
By Jerri Farris
ISBN: 1-59233-203-X
$12.00

10-Minute Energy-Saving
Secrets
By Jerri Farris
ISBN: 1-59233-245-5
$12.00